Acts of Forgiveness

T0048320

Acts of Forgiveness

Faith Journeys of a Gay Priest

TED KARPF

Foreword by Ray L. Hart

Box 611, Jefferson, North Carolina 28640
www.toplightbooks.com

LIBRARY OF CONGRESS CATALOGUING-IN-PUBLICATION DATA

Library of Congress Cataloging-in-Publication Data
Names: Karpf, Ted, 1948– author.
Title: Acts of forgiveness : faith journeys of a gay priest /
Ted Karpf ; foreword by Ray L. Hart.
Description: Jefferson, North Carolina : Toplight, 2019. |
Includes bibliographical references and index.
Identifiers: LCCN 2019041224 | ISBN 9781476679594
(softcover : acid free paper) ∞
ISBN 9781476637587 (ebook)
Subjects: LCSH: Karpf, Ted, 1948– | Episcopal Church—Clergy—
Biography. | Homosexuality—Religious aspects—Episcopal Church.
Classification: LCC BX5995.K37 A3 2019 | DDC 283.092 [B]—dc23
LC record available at https://lccn.loc.gov/2019041224

BRITISH LIBRARY CATALOGUING DATA ARE AVAILABLE

Front cover: Ted Karpf (Rick Saul Photography)

Printed in the United States of America

Toplight is an imprint of McFarland & Company, Inc., Publishers

Jefferson, North Carolina

To Selene Ember Rose Roberts
and her parents Deborah Michelle
and Jeremy Lee Roberts
and her uncle David Warren Karpf
and in Loving Memory
of Jean Evelyn Karpf
and James A. Munson

Table of Contents

"The way forward is to remember the past ... and then act."
—Street worker, Khayelitsha Township,
Cape Town, South Africa, 2001

Foreword
by Ray L. Hart

Early in his astonishing work *The Book of Disquiet*, Fernando Pessoa (in what he self-describes as a "factless autobiography") says that one writes or expresses something "to conserve its virtue and diminish its terror." This insight is itself conserved—without diminishing its own terror—with wholly vivacious power by Ted Karpf in this book, his overwhelming narrative (memoir) of the particularities (or, to use the medieval designation, *heccecieties*) of his own lived existence, brought under intensely thoughtful review and vitalization in the present.

Karpf brings up to two subjects for review in his narrative enterprise, that of the divine (God), and that of the human creature, who, as image of God, echoes the paradoxes and contradictions rendered present in the concrete determinacies of human existence. In my own reader response to this powerful text, I have been helped by two classical theoretical constructs (not mentioned by the author).

The first is Rudolf Otto's *The Idea of the Holy* (*Das Heilige*): The realized presence of the Holy is alluring, fascinating and attractive, while at the same time it is daunting, horrifying and repelling; and the same is true of all finite, human relationships. The second is Augustine's *Confessions*, which established autobiography as a distinctive genre of literature. The *Confessions* is a long prayer, addressed to one whom he did not know, but to one, he was convinced, had always known him, and thus was the guarantor of the Truth about him. Thus he asks of every person/thing he has known how he was known by them. Such an enter-

1

prise involves memory and the three modes of time. Memory, he says, is time present of things past.

If the things that happened in the past are left in the past, they will fester in the filter of values I had when they happened, and thus will function as fate. But if things past are revivified in the present, through which I now value them, the power of the past is broken, and I (and God) are free to get on with my life in the Eternal Now (i.e., the past is *redeemable*). So my response to Karpf's masterful narrative is that of Petrarch to his reading to the *Confessions* (to the effect): "I read the Confessions to know about another man's life and was rewarded by discovering my own." And/or the wisdom in Goethe's dictum: "Destiny has a way of denying us what we want in order to grant us what we need."

Ray L. Hart is emeritus professor of philosophical and systematic theology at Boston University; past dean, School of Theology (1999–2009); past chairman, Department of Religion; past director, Division of Religious and Theological Studies, Boston University. He received his Ph.D. from Yale and is the author of *Unfinished Man and the Imagination* (2001) and *God Being Nothing* (2016).

Preface

Kind reader—

This is a memoir about God: my dealings with God, or perhaps this is better stated as God's dealings with me over the course of a lifetime. While it focuses on the events of my life, most of all it is a God Story. As memoir, it is a retelling through my life's experiences as I have seen them related to God, but not exclusively so. Or perhaps it is simply a recollection or reflection of the awareness of something more than me at work in my life, rather than through immediate knowledge or apprehension of God in any given moment. Admittedly, there are a great number of things to remember and of which give an account. In addition, I have a spent a lifetime coming to terms with God—or what I understand or perceive to be God—through observation, study, and service. Finally, it must be said that early on in life, before I had words, I knew I was in love with God for reasons which shall be explained across these pages. Because this God Story is also about my life and my times, I am best situated to relate the story.

The approach to writing this work is heavily influenced by my years living and working in Africa, particularly South Africa, where I learned that past, present and future are often combined into Now. That is, the past is never really past as it is always influencing the present, and the future is being formulated by the choices made in every moment. Thus you will find that the chronology of my life is curiously commingled with past, present and future, creating my Now. This approach can be challenging, so I have used dates, times and places to locate you, reader, in the facts of my life, but that these events shape my present moment is without a doubt my working daily reality.

I am a Christian (my faith journey began in the Methodist church) and a priest, having served in the Episcopal Church for more than 36 years, though I was ordained in Holy Orders as clergy nearly five decades ago. My memories focus on those moments when God was obviously present or peculiarly distant to me through the rigors of human experience. There is no gloss on this text, which encapsulates a lifetime filled with longings for wholeness, yearnings for union or connection to the divine, contradictions to traditional belief, affirmations of unconditional love, lessons on the power of forgiveness, struggles under the overpowering burden of guilt and shame, and the utter pathos of living with sorrow and tragedy against a backdrop of being born in the mid–twentieth century and being gay in the Church. These moments of insight and struggle have emerged from my lifetime of service and doubt.

I am documenting my knowledge of God. It is incomplete, yet I have found it to be consistent for me and to be the absolute ground of consciousness to the core of my being. Through God and God's people I have learned that I am a person of fundamental worth—inclusive of inconceivable shame and liberating absolution—enabling me to love fully and passionately and to move forward in the recognition that all opposites are ultimately reconciled and united into one in the Great Mystery. As such, the Great Mystery cannot be solved as much as acknowledged. Because of my need for forgiveness for myself and my inherent brokenness, incompleteness is the given state of my condition and, I believe, is not fundamentally different for all humanity. This memoir describes the struggle of being a man who is at once a grandfather, a father, a son, a former spouse of both a woman and a man, a priest, a teacher, an administrator, a public servant, but most importantly a friend, who has spent his life trying to be faithful with integrity. At the heart of this story is a man who wishes to know God and live fully into the heart of God.

On the face of it, any life is paradoxical, loaded with contradictions and challenges with uncertain resolutions. Human dealings with God are also often paradoxical, not so much because God is necessarily paradoxical or that God really changes per se, as much as we change in our understanding, perception, and receptivity to depth and breadth of God and each other. Most of the time we cannot and do not think of ourselves as saints; rather, we tend to live fully and grotesquely into our brokenness. Thus I must describe myself as faltering and faithful, trusting and doubtful, vulnerable and stubborn, resilient and yet curiously fragile. I am a person who is just trying to figure out what it means to be able to embrace the opposites which are both God and us.

I am inviting you to look into my life with me. There you will neither find "Father Friendly" nor the "Devil's Disciple," though there are elements of both, and I will be vilified or condemned by some either way. I have found myself steering far from the path of faith while cleaving to the very heart of faith. At its core, my story simply documents what it means to live faithfully, boldly, and discreetly with integrity in a world of horrors and delights, surprises and affirmations, temptation and repulsion, confirmation and contradiction. Please join me in following and learning from this journey.

I

Home Going

Home is the place where, when you have to go there,
They have to take you in.
—Robert Frost, "The Death of the Hired Man"

I am home today. It has taken a lifetime to reach this place, which is both a geographic location and a state of being. The place is northern New Mexico—specifically the region between Santa Fe and Tierra Amarilla, the space between the Jemez and Sangre de Cristo mountain ranges—which is where I first fell in love with the earth and sky, now nearly 50 years ago. This land of this place is the High Desert of northern New Mexico (more formally called the Chihuahuan Desert, or *Desierto Chihuahuense*), which starts at 6,000 feet above sea level, with mountains rising up to 13,000 feet, replete with burnished dusty-brown plateaus covered by miles of sagebrush, tumbleweeds, chamisa, and Spanish sage as well as many of the region's trees: juniper, piñon, ponderosa pine, pecan, cottonwood, box elder, mountain mahogany, and cedar.

Its natural monuments are cast from the Chinle Formation of shale, forming red rock—the shade of dried blood—barren mesas created in the Triassic Period, accented by the Jurassic Entrada bone-white sandstone buttes. The mountains, whose peaks range from 9,000 to 13,000 feet above sea level, are predominantly alpine and evergreen, revealing the natural burn scars by its vast aspen meadows, some more than a hundred years old, that quake in spring, summer, and fall. This land was also once covered by a Cretaceous inland sea, which is part of the deep and primordial emotional and spiritual draw to this land for me.

One can only imagine a world where the tops of mountains today once formed the bottom of that sea, and where one can still find ancient remains of underwater sand dunes, marine plants, and chambered nautiluses or other sea creatures on the mountaintops. These rock formations are a testament to the many peoples who have more recently passed through here, with their ancient petroglyphs and modern graffiti. Each symbol, a silent witness.

The crystalline cobalt blue skies host a daily light show of banded colors at sunrise and sunset, with cloud displays that are among the most variable and exotic in the world. The overall impact of this dramatic environment impinges on me constantly, compelling me to feel rather small and insignificant while simultaneously being totally caught up in the spaciousness of the vast countryside. Whether I am in the mountains or in the desert, I see life in its grandeur and finitude. At its core, though, it is always about the survival of the fittest. Being fit, however, does not ensure survival per se, as much as it simply gives one a fighting chance. Fitness, though, is not merely a matter of physical or muscular development or necessarily good health, but is a place of mental maturity to a point where one can embrace the known and unknown with equanimity. I say this as one who has been living with a variety of health challenges, which I will address more fully later.

Because this environment is so present in all interactions—from the sultry warmth of a summer evening to the refreshing coolness of a mountain autumn morning, from the darkening of the sky ripped by the frantic winds of a monsoon rain to the frosty snow of a winter morning—I stay attuned to the seasons, the colors, as well as to the more subtle changes in the local flora and fauna. I cannot escape the immediacy of the environment or how it announces the presence of God in all of my dealings.

Likewise, under the burden of a historic legacy of the use and abuse of land and the conquests and tragedies of its many peoples over the past thousand years, there is a grotesque undercurrent of racial, cultural, ethnic, and familial violence which compels me to face the brutality of relationships fraught by sin and brokenness from which there is often no escape. Perhaps it is the fact of simply being "up against it" in every possible way—physically and emotionally, culturally and racially, environmentally and personally—that I find this land to be an aphrodisiac and stimulant as much as depressant and discouragement, each and every day. Such is the land which I call "home" and in which I encounter God.

Home: The States of Being

A state of being, home is that place where they have to take you in no matter what you've done, or so I have been told. I have no kinfolk here. I have no lineage or implicit claim to the history of this particular land. I am very much the product of the assimilators who came to America all the way into the mid–twentieth century. Thus, I often find myself feeling like a dislocated foreigner, whose forebears came to this country as recently as 1905 during the Jewish diaspora from Europe and 1910 during the Irish diaspora. I am also a descendant of those who arrived on this continent as early as 1620 on a small boat from England. I have paternal and maternal roots in all those tribes. What America is, of which no other place can lay such claim, is the absolute assimilation of previously warring factions into one family called Americans. Perhaps because of the sojourning lives of my forebears, or maybe in spite of them, I came to be dislocated from their cultures and traditions as is the wont of many Americans. And yet these roots in those disparate traditions have been the tendrils leading to my own self-discovery and the recovery of my soul. When you are from nowhere in particular—as one who was born in one place, grew up in another, educated in yet another, and worked professionally in many others—you come from everywhere and can lay claim only to that which you decide to call "home." Spending much of my life on the road, particularly the last 30 years of working and traveling and becoming a citizen of the world, I have come to call northern New Mexico and the wild places of the Chama River Valley—the Chama River being a tributary of the mighty Rio Grande fed by the seasonal runoff of the Rio del Oso and Rio Ojo Caliente—my home. This area of the ancient seabed will one day be the place where I will make my final repose. The land, the wind, the harmonics of the rock formations, the rivers and streams echo with sounds and images that cause me to revert to my earliest memories of life. And yet I only found this place in my twenties. To many, it is known as the land of O'Keeffe and cowboys, but it is also the land of traditional tribal dancers from the Pueblo peoples, descendants of the "lost" people of the Anasazi, as well as of mystics who still roam through its mountains and valleys, cleverly disguised as "locals," whether they be farmers, *brujos* and *brujas*, ranchers, lost hippies, Orthodox monks, turbaned Sikhs, Hindu gurus and babas, Yogi guides, Buddhist monks and roshis, or Baptist preachers. They are all here and more. The lesson of being here is learning to recognize them.

The High Desert is often a place of great violence, in large part due to the constant, hard-fought struggle by humans contending with the hostile environments of desert and heat, wind and occasional drenching floods, mountainous highlands and lush verdant lowlands in the river valleys, and arid arroyos awaiting the sweetness of snowmelt and monsoon rain. The physical and psychological tension of this drama have profoundly spiritual edges, if one is open to them, which tends to call one out, forcing the soul on its impoverished self and ultimately upon God. Into such a wild place and in this very specific way, I have repeatedly sojourned over the years to the core of my own soul and its dogged grasp on my often paltry faith. I have been among the very fortunate to have always rediscovered the God of my understanding at the end of my rope, with reverence and awe. This God is the very ground of my Being, whose essence is consciousness itself. This consciousness is non-local—that is, not based in physical manifestations like a physical body—but also omnipresent, life-giving and life-sustaining, gracious and brutal in unwavering honesty. Thus, to be at home is to be a soul in union with the Great Soul of all of life. There is a gospel song which seems to say it better:

> When peace, like a river, attendeth my way,
> When sorrows like sea billows roll;
> Whatever my lot, Thou hast taught me to say,
> It is well, it is well with my soul.
> (Refrain)
> It is well with my soul,
> It is well, it is well with my soul.

Spending much of my lifetime searching for "home," I came to settle here in my last stage of life because no matter where I was in the world, northern New Mexico was the place to which I always returned. Yes, I have close friends here and had one in particular who is of this land, but I also have friends everywhere I have lived and worked. I have come to be comfortable, no matter where I am. But here in northern New Mexico, I have sojourned far and wide into the mountains and valleys, in wildernesses and barren plains, and have always managed to go deep within myself and return alive to tell of it. I always found myself at the end of the road to be at home here. Those who have known me know that I have often waxed romantic about northern New Mexico. Perhaps such unreal romanticism has been a way of keeping others at bay— "Nothing could be that good," they might be heard to say—or as a way of covering the dark places and contradictions about life here. Regardless, I am at home, for better or worse.

Stewardship and Sharing

For all my love and passion for this place, even after decades of engagement with it, I underestimated the sheer power of the environment and the interplay of the raw powers of ethnicity, culture, history, and tradition when it came to owning land here. In 2014, I retired to a small farm/ranch (11 acres), upcountry near Georgia O'Keeffe's home in Abiquiú. This land is jointly owned with a deeply beloved friend and colleague, José; I purchased half of the land in 2004 as a way of helping him make a major career change from academia and public service to full-time priesthood. We first met in public health work during my three-year (1989–1992) stint with the U.S. Public Health Service (USPHS). He worked for the State of New Mexico's Health Department Stop AIDS program, in the bars and gay gathering places across the state, while I was the regional HIV/AIDS liaison specialist with the USPHS, organizing five states to do HIV prevention and treatment work. I confess that I fell in love with him the day we met. It was not so much sexual as it was emotional, intellectual, and spiritual. His quiet energy and my kinetic energy strangely complemented one another. I could challenge him, charging him up, and he did the same with me, calming me down to listen. We shared our deepest fears and greatest joys and found ways to meet up over nearly a decade.

He is Hispanic—that is, descended directly from the first Spanish

After mass, conversation between Ted and José's parents.

conquistadors of the New World in the 1600s. I, on the other hand, am an Anglo-Jew, and our differing cultures came to play themselves out. When I returned to full-time church work in the early 1990s, I would make my bi-annual retreats at the Monastery of Christ in the Desert, 34 miles above Abiquiú. His home and land were located between Santa Fe and Abiquiú. So I found myself passing by or stopping in, either going or coming from the monastery. Because his greeting was always "mi casa es su casa" (my home is your home), I soon found myself staying at his house for my retreats. Because he would often be on the road for days at a time, I usually had the house to myself. The land there was rich and alive, next to the same river as the monastery, but the convenience of being at "home" far outweighed the rather mean monk's cell and the rigors of the abbey with its rather poor cuisine. I liked cooking for myself and enjoyed the silence which I found there. Besides, I was deeply drawn to my friend and his insistence on educating me about culture and tradition. Over our many years of association I hosted his aging parents and siblings in Washington at the National Cathedral and periodically celebrated mass—even though I am not Roman Catholic—in their family *capilla* (chapel) outside of Santa Fe.

This "home place," as I called it, is about 60 miles northwest of Santa Fe, located just below a ruin of an ancient pueblo from the 1500s, and adjoining a number of small farms and ranches, some occupied by descendants of well-known historic New Mexican land-grant families. Other occupants included a rich mixture of more newly arrived Hispanics, Pueblo natives, and persons of mixed blood, along with a few of us

José and Ted in the family *capilla* during better days.

Anglos, who settled among these variously indigenous peoples. The property was a small piece of a large single-family farm, one of the descendants of which was still a neighbor. By the mid–twentieth century the soil had begun to give out, yielding to fragile economics and poor crops. Lying fallow for some years, it had become an excellent location for limited horse and cattle grazing due to its proximity to the river, which never dries up.

On his portion of the land, my friend had a natural adobe home, which he had constructed with family and friends over three years. It was of basic design and construction, built of very economical materials, which after nearly 20 years were failing. Because of my long association with the land and periodic occupancy of the home, I wanted to settle there in retirement for as long as my precarious health would hold out. (I have been struggling with congestive heart failure and failing kidneys and liver for some years.) Even with the rundown condition of the house, which I knew required renovation and upgrading to be habitable in all seasons, I saw it as a challenge and an opportunity to restore the adobe structure and steward the land back into more productive possibilities. He agreed. So together we planned my retirement there in 2012, beginning the renovations in the summer of 2013.

My piece of the land, purchased nine years before, was located on some 600 feet of riverfront on the Chama River, just above where it joins the Rio Grande on its journey through New Mexico from Colorado. Water—rivers and streams—are the life-blood of New Mexico. Without these waters, life would not be possible. To further enhance the power of water, more than 400 years ago the invading Spanish conquerors introduced a system of irrigation ditches through what the Spanish called an *acequia*. These large ditches draw the water off the river, moving it through a series of hand-dug ditches on each farm, which in turn is flooded by the water moving over the land, thereby returning the water to the river miles downstream. To maintain this fragile system, everyone along the *acequia*—which is several miles long where the home place is—must maintain the walls of the main ditch and the ones on the farm, cleaning it of weeds and roots, which tend to take up life in the moist earth. This is done each spring. Thus, to maintain the *acequia* is, in fact, to maintain life itself.

One of the most efficient ways to clean the *acequia* of weeds and

The land of the "home place" in Medanales, New Mexico.

to harden the dirt/clay walls is to burn the ditch. Each year, throughout early Lent in northern New Mexico, residents along an *acequia* cut, rake, and burn their particular section of the ditch, and then clean and burn their smaller farm ditches all the way down into the fields. It is truly a trial by fire as one can easily spend six to ten hours in the ditches running across the land. Anticipating the rising of the river due to snowmelt and rain, in the middle of March the whole community gathers to remove the overgrowth around the main *acequia* which feeds all the adjoining farms and ranches, and to clean those sections where the residential owners are too infirm or are living away from the land. It is a sacred responsibility and the means of bonding with the land and the larger *pueblo*—the community.

Also on our shared piece of land, nurtured by the water pouring over it, is a grove of 300-year-old apple and pear trees brought here by the *conquistadors* and their inheritors. These trees are a testament to a land with very deep roots. Part of my challenge of settling there was to take over stewarding and pruning the trees, which had gone unmanaged for nearly a decade. In the course of the spring of 2014, I found myself, with an eager couple who worked for me, pruning nearly two tons of limbs and overgrowth, as well as clearing the orchard of volunteer trees and shrubs. The pile of debris was mountainous, and on the weekend of the annual ditch-burning, we also burned this pile. It took six hours to burn through and two days to clear. The ashes of the past were then buried in newly turned soil, enriching everything in the grove.

Trouble in Eden

Shortly after I had fully moved into the newly renovated house in late February 2014, José appeared for a day, seemingly delighted at what I had done with the house to make it my home. He remarked then that he did not intend to return to this place for up to decade or more, being younger and in much better physical shape than I. I expected I would be literally long gone by then, so our verbal arrangement of my living in and caring for the house and land until he came home worked for both of us, or so I believed.

Something changed. In mid–April I was greeted with a letter from a lawyer notifying me that I was being "evicted from the premises" on the 18th of June. I reached out shortly thereafter but my friend did not respond to letters, emails, or telephone entreaties where I offered to meet him and discuss what led to this precipitous and drastic decision and to determine how we could reach an equitable solution. I had spent all my retirement bonus and life savings and indebted myself to the bank to pay for the renovations and changes required to meet state building codes. The lack of clarity or conversation, the sudden change of heart, the open distrust of even communicating—this was not anything our relationship had ever experienced in more than two decades. The ghosts of my past—the sting of betrayals, the violence and brutality of parents, rejection by a lover and subsequently mutual friends, divorce, dissolution, and disorder—all came forth as wraiths from another life, haunting me while I was dealing with this unexplained event. (You will learn more about these in subsequent chapters.) The multiple nightmares of loss—of one whom I presumed to be a very close friend, of permanent housing, of a major investment loss—dragged on for months.

I was grateful when, at the urging of friends, I finally sought and hired legal counsel in Santa Fe. My attorney immediately found legal precedent for me to have done what I did; that is, trust an oral agreement (contract) based on an extensive history with a friend. Such matters—which notoriously go wrong, I later learned—had been successfully tried and tested in the New Mexico courts, but not without a great deal of time and protracted expense. Without even the willingness of my friend to discuss or negotiate or explain the hows and whys of our situation, I was still at a loss as to what the next step would be. It quickly became evident, though, that I would lose in a local court in my up-country county; the case would publicly appear to be a simple matter of Anglo versus Hispanic, indigenous local versus East Coast outsider, Episcopal (Protestant) priest versus Roman Catholic priest. Such are the conditions to be considered when assuming or relying on the strength of local justice.

Because some of my friend's friends and contacts reacted strongly and even passionately about the "apparent injustice" of my claim to the land, they appeared on the property, carrying firearms. I was quickly advised by legal counsel to vacate the premises under the cloak of secrecy. My friend's friends were lifelong members of the indigenous community, where violence as a means of settling disputes has been a way of life for generations. It was deemed too dangerous for me to live there safely; I couldn't agree more. While I was not overtly threatened with firearms, the thinly veiled threats and ongoing harassment of cars pulling up to the house both during the day and at night, with people getting out of said cars and trucks and walking around for hours, watching me and the property for 35 days and nights, led me and my legal team to determine that it was time to vacate. After my rushed departure in 18 hours, I then filed suit, agreeing to let the courts do what they do, pending appeals to the Supreme Court of New Mexico, if that became necessary.

The brutal legal processes continued over the rest of that summer, leading to court filings and countersuits. To solve it quickly, a new judge—this time at the state capital in Santa Fe—was insistent that evidence of mediation was required before any further legal process could go forward. José and I then went through something more akin to arbitration than mediation, responding to a third-party lawyer without seeing one another, sitting with our own legal counsel in separate rooms for an entire day in late August 2014. I received a settlement of 25 cents on the dollar, which would preclude any further litigation and running up any additional costs, which I really couldn't afford.

Through the arbitration process, though, I learned that a third party—a local indigenous Hispanic rancher who had been grazing cattle for free on the land for nearly ten years and who wanted my land—had started this conflict. Under an unusual clause in New Mexico Territorial Law, when land "appears to have been abandoned," the party grazing animals and even minimally repairing fences can legally lay claim to it. I had been away nearly nine years before renovating the house. My portion of the land, with its water access to the river, became the object of both desire and contention to this rancher. He had manipulated my friend into believing that, because of the home improvements, I was about to lay claim to his land. Curiously, no one factored in the fact that my life expectancy is considerably shorter than the requisite decade. Because of the bonds of blood, shared culture, and heritage, our friendship of 25 years had become expendable. History between us was of no account. Trust was shattered. And all oral agreements abandoned. Jealousy and fear have a way of corrupting the best of friendships, even between two Christian priests.

Going Home

I had suddenly found myself inhabiting a place where I was not only unwelcome but where a 25-year friendship had been abolished with the stroke of a pen and without mutual face-to-face consultation during the mediation. Stunned at the emotional and spiritual loss as much as by the loss of a home and a reduction in already scarce financial resources, I was like a dead man negotiating a gravesite. While I was profoundly attached to the land where I had worshipped and prayed for more than a decade and on which I had just expended all my financial worth to improve and stabilize, it was now all gone, with the exception of my paid-for deeded acreage by the river and the easement through the whole ranch to get there. Perhaps this experience was a metaphor for all of life: Nothing lasts.

I had accumulated a grand total of 120 days of actual habitation and savored every day of being there, as well as the 60 days of preparation and renovation. Living in Santa Fe since that time, I can always look up the Rio Grande Valley toward Abiquiú, and I confess that I still feel very melancholy about the whole situation. But I am much more aware of the impact and crosscurrents of race and ethnicity as they play themselves out in even the most intimate and long-term relationships. The inherent ubiquitous violence of this land and its peoples is no longer a story I tell; it is a breathing reality of what can and does go wrong in the most basic of relationships. Blood—whether it be real kin or assumed kin—is indeed thicker than water, especially when congealed in culture and tradition bonded with historic blood vendettas and generations of distrust and abuse.

I have also come to know that home—my home—as place is not so much about the very ground itself—though I occasionally long for it—as much as it is about the area or region where the light and darkness daily play across the evening sky, where the winds blow freely and sometimes even fiercely on a cold winter day. And where the seasonal changes are marked with new growth, fruition, and finally dormancy or death. I am at home, in that I am among beloved friends with whom I trust my very life. To be here in northern New Mexico again, I had to face the harsh fact that one day in this relatively small city and state capital of New Mexico, I will see my former friend and will—by calling and necessity—greet him in peace. I have prayed for the means of forgiveness for the wrong committed against me; not so much because I believe there is a future with him, as it is clear there is not. Rather, I have had to learn to pray—again—for the means of forgiveness, allowing myself to have a future. And it remains such to this day. The doors and windows of my home remain physically wide open without locks and bars, for there is little now that I possess that would grieve me if it were to disappear. I determined that home would be a place which provided safety and openness, welcome and solitude, sanctity and laughter. To this day, it does.

Where was God in the midst of all this horror? God was present. That is all I can say with any conviction. I know this because I had a recurrent dream. This dream began on the second day after receiving the notice of eviction. In the dream I heard the voice of my former mentor and confessor, Archbishop Desmond Tutu. While it was his voice, it was not Desmond per se whom I was hearing. I perceived that it was God speaking through him to me.

As the dream opens, I am at the home place. The voice addresses me in Desmond's characteristic giggle. "So, Teddy, how is it going in your retirement? Did you move into the house and renovate it according your best standards?"

"Your Grace," I answer, "I have and it is wonderful. It has everything I ever imagined. And I have the solitude I have needed and prayed about for so long."

Then he laughs uproariously. "Isn't God good? Isn't God very good!" Then he asks, "Teddy, did you get to pray in the way you had hoped and are you in constant communication with God?"

"Oh yes, your Grace," I answer. "I am spending several hours a day praying and contemplating the wonders of what God is doing here in this glorious bit of creation."

"Oh," he observes, "isn't God good? Isn't God exceedingly good!" Then a third question: "Teddy, are you doing everything that you had hoped you would do at this time in your life?"

I hesitate as I feel the ground falling beneath me. "Yes, your Grace, I am doing exactly what I had hoped that I would do."

"Oh, Teddy, isn't God very very good?" Gales of laughter follow, then a sudden deafening silence. "So now that you have gotten to do all that you wanted to do and have prayed in the way you wanted to pray and have the home that you always imagined … isn't it time to do what God wants you to do?"

That dream haunted me for the next five months, until I agreed to go to Buffalo, New York, to serve as interim priest in a parish that was in more difficulty than it knew. It was the winter of 2014–15, one of the worst then on record with 123.4 inches of snow and subzero temperatures for three months. I found myself able to throw my whole self into this place of strangers whom I'd not sought to impress or even endear. They became my new community, one of healing and hope, allowing me the space to find myself in the midst of my confusion and self-doubt. They gave me the gifts of overwhelming affirmation and trust, thereby granting me the means of healing—that is, of mending a deeply broken heart and repairing my shattered dreams of home. While there, I learned

Celebrating the sacrament of Holy Baptism, Easter Day 2015, Trinity Episcopal Church, Buffalo, New York.

that my maternal great-great-grandfather had had a lucrative business there—within view of my office—in the 1870s. He was buried just up the street in the city's Forest Lawn Cemetery, final resting place for the great and near great. So I had curiously stumbled into a previously unknown home of my own family.

The parish's journey, which had begun in April 2013, ended with the arrival of their new permanent priest in summer 2015. My time with them lasted nine months. I call it my "journey to wholeness" because it was where I rediscovered my gifts and graces as a priest, and my strengths and weaknesses as a man among a group of total strangers. I was able to not only hear the voice of God among them, but be the presence of God to a wounded people. The healing was clearly mutual. This winter desert of my life became the place where spring could and would eventually come and then I could at last go home, alive and well.

And so today I reside in Santa Fe, nurtured by close friends and the abiding land and sky. I live quietly and say mass occasionally at the local parish. Periodically, I find myself in the midst of my avocation in community engagement around health and healthcare, particularly educating others about death and dying, and am constantly preoccupied with observing the skies, testing the winds, watching the movement of animals and birds and, of course, writing daily. In other ways, I spend time contemplating the wonder of God and the whole creation as well as my own life lived. Home is finally where all of this now happens for me.

II

Forgiveness and Loving

Sometimes ... a wave of light breaks into our darkness, and it is as though a voice were saying: "You are accepted. You are accepted." Accepted by that which is greater than you, and the name of which you do not know. Do not ask for the name now; perhaps you will find it later. Do not try to do anything now; perhaps later you will do much....

In the light of this grace we perceive the power of grace in our relation to others and to ourselves. We experience the grace of being able to look frankly into the eyes of another, the miraculous grace of reunion of life with life.
—Paul Tillich, *The Shaking of the Foundations: Sermons*

"So how do I forgive?" I was speaking to Father John after being fired from a church and removed from an appointed post in the diocese—all by the same bishop and all on the same day. I was to see Father John ostensibly to make my regular confession. In June 1984, the bishop of Fort Worth, the Right Rev. A. Donald Davies, refused to support my work at Christ the King parish—which began in 1982. I had a two-year-old at home and a working spouse, and now I was to be immediately unemployed. The only reason given by the bishop was that I was "not good for the parish, and we no longer have need of you in this diocese." Then he sent me out with this advice: "You will have to go elsewhere to be a priest."

I had been editor of the diocesan paper and assistant secretary of the diocese. I was now out in the cold, sent into the ecclesiastical equivalent of outer darkness. For the first time, the notion of confession and coming to terms with the brutality of life on these new terms, Christian terms—namely, being forgiving—had to become lifestyle in this moment, and provide a way of being in the world. No one warned me that anything like this could or would ever happen as a priest. After all, the bishop is considered one's spiritual father or mother, and the Church is home! Now I was being cast out. I had a difficult time determining how this entrance into the life of the Episcopal Church brought me to this place.

The Cost of Loving

Years of therapy had gotten me to the level of understanding that I had been brutally abused in my parents' home, from birth through adolescence. The psychological abuse extended well into adulthood, until I ordered my father out of my home for his ongoing harassment. This happened only months before the encounter with the bishop. I was 34 years old. My father thought of me as an outspoken hypocrite for being a priest, a view he held of all professional practitioners of religion, and often said so. My mother disliked priests in general due to her upbringing with an aunt who was a nun. Between them, there was little understanding or regard for what I was professionally, not to mention who I was as their son. My father fueled his anger by goading me about the Church, faith, religion, and those who practice it, including me. It was too much, taking me back to a time of his abuse by using me for a target while teaching me tennis when I was a young boy. I asked him to stop the verbal abuse; he didn't. I then demanded that he leave my home. He slammed his hand down on the dining room table, stating, "I will never return to your home until you apologize." I never did. He died nine years later. We were still estranged. I didn't cry. I didn't weep. I was more surprised and hurt by the demand from my mother, echoed by my youngest brother, at the time of the funeral. Each said, "Don't come. We don't want you here." At the service, the same brother announced that my father had only two sons, the two younger brothers. Those in attendance reported their discomfort at these words, for some had come to be with me, the eldest son, and I was not present at my own father's funeral.

With Father John I was able to verbalize my feelings, breaking into a rage about my sudden and unfair predicament with the bishop. I was feeling the same betrayal and estrangement that I had known between

The Karpf brothers (left to right): Ted (8 years), Tim (3 years), and Bud (6 years), at home at Christmas, 1956.

my father and me. But Father John's expected sympathy didn't come; instead, he asked me to forgive the bishop. I turned the question around and demanded that he tell me how. His answer, simple and direct, was: "Pray for him until you love him."

My mouth was agape in incredulity and disbelief. "Until I love him? Are you kidding?" I had not reckoned with forgiveness in my rage at the unfairness of things, and now particularly as he was suggesting that forgiveness would have to become a way of life. It was too early in my process of coming to terms with things. This kind of personal instruction, bordering on therapy in the confessional, was really a form of spiritual direction. It was, I came to realize later, less confessional and more operational. My whole world was being challenged, and this man, this priest, was directing me to forgive. This was not what I wanted to hear. I wanted to have time to rant and rave about the injustices inflicted on me, to feel his sympathy, and to listen to his righteous indignation mimicking mine.

Quietly and gently he took my hand and said, "Yes, until you love him."

"That's a good deal more than forgiveness," I insisted. "That's an extra mile of appreciation and embrace to someone who has deeply wronged me. I am afraid that I cannot perfect it or even have the desire to offer it in this life. And that is a very long time."

"Then you must pray for him and for you to one day love him," he offered. And so began a decades-long period of praying and forgiving (as I have been forgiven by God) until this day. Over the course of my life, I have been repeatedly challenged by difficult or unfair, unjust, or contrary people. In each case I have had to practice the forgiveness I could not readily offer, but had to learn to offer it, over and over again. It is the nature of what I hold to be true about faith—forgiveness is the core of the Christian experience. Forgiving as I have been forgiven— for God has forgiven me repeatedly—is the way I have come to terms with forgiveness.

Therapy and Forgiveness

Along the way, over the years, I have done more than forgive. I have prayed for the most offensive of my detractors and personal enemies. It is as if the lesson needs to be lived and re-lived, over and over again, across a life, until it becomes a natural act instead of the unnatural act that it seemed to me to be.

While I was a graduate student in theological training, I underwent three years of therapeutic analysis. It was a painful endeavor, yet it was only my initial entrance into the therapeutic process. From that work I learned that therapy is alchemy. We—the therapist and I—could turn the dross of my life into gold. That is, the garbage of pain, disgrace, shame, and guilt could be turned into assets for living. It was not an easy or comfortable journey by any standard. What had begun in a therapist's office at age 24 continued on and off for another 30 years, and there was still more after that, until I was certified as a Gestalt therapist, along with being trained as a spiritual director. Each time in therapy I discovered that it is more like peeling an onion than shredding a soul. But it has qualities of both. Each new situation brings new challenges and dimensions of the damage of childhood and early adulthood. Each major choice I have made and am still making is a reflection of my "in the moment" mental, emotional, and spiritual state with all the history attached and, hopefully, illumined. Each significant person in my life has, at one time or another, demanded that I look upon them, through the hurt and outrage they have inflicted, with empathy and forgiveness, with gratitude and acceptance, and always with respect. Many times I have failed to get it in the proper sequence.

After the breakup of my 14-year relationship with my partner Buck in 2000, I underwent PTSD therapy and weekly acupuncture treatment to deal with the effects of grief. I was counseled through the loss to recount all the good things that had happened in the relationship and the good things that I had brought into it. It took me months to find any. In the meantime, I raged on and on about the deceptions and disconnects that we suffered at each other's hands. I replayed all the abandonments I had known in my life. I ate at the table of despair, gnawing on the bones of the past, mostly mine. It would be years of praying for forgiveness of the one who had taken my heart and life for granted and lured me out of my calling and profession for love of him, yet who could abandon me for another—someone who was already taken in a relationship. With each day of our breaking up, something that took six months in all, I found myself vainly and wantonly searching for deceptions and abandonments. I found them in great numbers and grieved them even more loudly. This was such a contrast to what had begun with my ending my married relationship to Kaye, my wife from 1975 through 1989. Where she and I had talked our way through it, carefully, intent on keeping each other's dignity and self-respect intact, Buck and I railed at one another about how each had hurt the other. Where Kaye and I owned our faults and missteps, Buck and I blamed and laid guilt upon each other while denying that there was any truth in what the other said. Where I left one love for another with sorrow and remorse, Buck was remorseless with his decision to declare his love for a man already committed to another. Where there was a dignified ending with Kaye, there was none between Buck and me.

Pleading with the universe for an explanation, I heard only long silences and stared blankly into the darkness, endlessly sobbing. Starving for love, I also starved myself of food, wishing to somehow complete the act of self-destruction by self-denial. I found myself totally bereft and empty. Everything I thought was true about my life and love seemed hollow and without form, and so it remained for several years after the actual breakup itself.

Failure to Love?

I believed that in both relationships (with Kaye and Buck) I had somehow failed miserably in loving and caring, in supporting and valuing. I often failed to see that I was also a victim in this situation, rather than merely a perpetrator, based often on my obsessions with my deficiencies and failures. I thought for too long that somehow I deserved to be abandoned. As I would come to learn: No one does! Fortunately, I was surrounded by those who loved me, in spite of what had happened, as they made themselves available through my long hours of crying and regretful self-recriminations. They were the arms of God granting me embrace for which I had longed and for which I prayed.

Because Archbishop Desmond Tutu knew that Buck and I were a

Gay Pride March to the Texas State Capitol in Austin: Buck (dark glasses) and Ted, 1989.

household, that we were no longer together for the two years that I had been in South Africa since 2001, I asked him, "How long do I pray for him?" His reply, "Until you love him." That was all he said. I was again flummoxed and frustrated. I had no inclination to pray for him; I wanted him to disappear. So that prayer took nearly a decade to pray as well, during which I often had to ask myself, "Is anything or anyone unforgivable?" I must respond, if I am to remain faithful to scripture, my faith, and experience, "Probably not. No, nothing and no one is beyond forgiveness, but learning to accept that fact, and gaining the stamina and will that it takes to do it, may well take a lifetime." I had to learn that loving did not mean approbation or romance or attraction, but a fair and honest assessment of a person and a willingness to not seek ill or woe for or toward that person in any way. Rather, it is crucial to seek a place of well-being and prosperity for the other. When my former partner returned and asked me to reconsider my relationship to him after more than a decade and a half of silence, I was able to say, "No, I will not be in relationship with you because you are toxic to me." It was a curious test of my own thinking and self-respect.

"That I have loved you with all my heart cannot be denied," I continued. "That I have long grieved the loss of you beyond measure, I must admit to that. I wish only well for you, but need to be without you for the remainder of this life. I will continue to pray for you daily because that is who I am."

My words were met with silence. He was never good at saying what or how he felt, and this time was no exception. All he could do was express frustration with my answer, telling me that he had changed, but I signaled that I would not hear it. Once again, silence, grudging silence ensued. It was not the answer that he wanted, but it was what I gave from the fullness of my being.

To forgive and be forgiven, as I learned from Desmond Tutu, is not to be without memory or forgetful about the past; rather, it is to be mindful of it, remembering it with fullness and detail, and then reaching through the pain of the memories to the reality that we are all flawed human beings. The pain is real. The losses are real. In that spirit, it is also true that there is a deep yearning within—some would call it "soul"—for connection and forgiveness. But the truth of what makes reconciliation possible is more often that the offended party recognizes that normalcy and balance in human relations requires forgiveness and healing to maintain the humanity of self as well as that of the other. As long as I am holding on to my anger and hurt, little movement is possible. I am doomed to reside in the past, curtailing any hope of the future. Indeed, some may seek forgiveness first, but praying for them, and praying for one's self to forgive, creates the environment where real forgiveness and acceptance are possible.

Acceptance and Growth

Real acceptance of another after an act of deception, a breach of trust, or break in relationship is to undergo the process of removing regret, dismissing desire, acknowledging guilt, rejecting recrimination, upholding justice, claiming mercy, and extending compassion. On the face of it, it is exhausting.

I have always found praying for another to be the beginning of acceptance and the hardest part of the journey to freedom. I have to move my ego from claiming my own hurt and righteousness to concern for the one who wounded me. It is difficult to hold grudges and harbor anger when you have brought the offending party to the proverbial "throne of grace" in prayer. This action of praying is about being transformed before you know that you are being transformed, and somehow in that journey your hurt is being healed.

There are no words really to describe the ongoing function of prayer and forgiveness other than to experience the alternating joy and sorrow of it firsthand. Even if prayer is nothing more than holding kind or good thoughts about another, it still has a salutary effect. It appears that it is the givenness of being human and alive. Why then are we always so surprised when something difficult, untoward, unfair, or even awful happens to us? "Because it is happening to *me!*" we surmise. "I always thought I would get off free" (that is, without pain or suffering) is as good an answer as I have been able to give.

The Power of Forgiveness

Much of my early life, as I now understand it, was characterized by protracted silences which articulated the lack of forgiveness by the most powerful people in my life then. My father would not forgive my mother for becoming pregnant with me out of wedlock. My mother would not forgive my being the product of that pregnancy, causing a premature marriage, with me being born at an inconvenient time, seven months after the wedding. It was the 1940s.

On their wedding day, February 14, 1948, Joan Shepherd and William "Bill" Karpf, Jr.

My parents would not forgive me their loss of sleep for being a colicky baby. Later they would not forgive me for being "different" before I had words to describe how or why I was different. My father would not forgive himself for acting or perhaps even feeling differently about other males in his over-attentiveness to them and his raw hatred and distrust of women. While not acting on his apparent inclination intentionally or directly, it was evident that he was deeply attracted to men and preferred their company when he sought them out over all interests for family. His insistence on touching me, inappropriately and often assaultively, only raised my level of speculation about him and his orientation later in life when I could actually understand it. My mother would not face his bitterness and usually turned his silence into her rage. Neither would she forgive her father for abandoning her at age seven, when her mother died of cholera in Greenwich Village in 1932. My father would not forgive his parents for being a Jew and Gentile couple in a time when both were more or less dead to their respective families for being of different tribes. He would not forgive his father for being poor after the stock market crash of 1929, when he was being indulged and spoiled rotten by an adoring grandmother. My mother would not forgive her stepmother for not being the mother she needed. Her father never told his new wife that he was the father of two daughters. However, that same stepmother would live in my mother's care until she was 101, and, for more than a quarter of a century, she depended on my mother alone for support. And neither of my parents could forgive my father's sister, my Aunt Jean, for wanting to adopt me as her own rather than watch them inflict more pain and suffering on me.

Aunty! Together for a lunch date are Jean E. Karpf and Ted in Dallas, October 2017.

Is it any wonder that I found that my

emotional life was full of holes and incompleteness, like a hunk of Swiss cheese? There were deep gaps in the fabric of my emotional, spiritual, and psychological well-being. I believed that I was merely taking up space and sucking air, but my background provided no insight as to how to deal with and negotiate my way through all sorts of emotionally laden situations. So it is perhaps a triumph of therapy, insightful mentors, fierce will, and a generous amount of compassion of friends and later from extended family that I became a supportive father, a loyal friend, and a faithful priest who is often addressed as "father." It is also the power of God to infuse life with the will for wholeness and then be present to deliver it.

Violence as Lifestyle

Violence seemed to be a way of life with my parents. They were so caught in their own helplessness and pain that they could not see their own actions or the consequences of their parenting for many, many years. Ameliorated by alcohol, my mother found that her beatings and rages on me provided a great emotional outlet. The therapeutic process initiated in seminary revealed my rage toward and deep fear of my parents' constant emotional abuse and brutal violence, which had become so normative in my life. It was not unusual to be beaten for virtually anything—from challenging my parents about their view of the world to my failure to do homework on time or correctly. Beatings usually ended with Mother being so exasperated with me when I fought back verbally. Her refrain would be something like, "If I could just tell you why you deserve this, but I can't." As years went by, I came to the conclusion that I was adopted; or worse, foisted off on them for some terrible reason. Kids do this in the face of the unknown. In therapy I learned of my emotional deficiencies and sheer rage due to the abuse of love and the inflicting of violence done in the name of that love.

In the therapist's office one day, he asked, "You've said little about family, particularly your mother. Would you like to tell me about it?" I really don't know what I said, but I do remember the feeling. At the end of the hour, the side table and lamp were smashed, and the arms of the chair broken. I walked out as if in a daze and descended the stairs to

Commonwealth Avenue and Kenmore Square, the location of his office near Boston University. I found a lamp pole and hung on for dear life as the whole world felt tilted and out of synch. Disoriented, I eventually found my way home and wept for hours. The following week, I thanked him and, with his new furniture in place, the work of therapy continued for two more years.

It was also during therapy that for the first time I admitted to another person my deep physical and emotional attraction to men. I discovered that in many ways this orientation was truly out of my control, despite my "experience" with women. Rather than letting it all come out on my father, who took on the role of emotional batterer in their relationship, each of my parents worked their violence on each other to such a point that they both went after me whenever they felt the slightest justification of their various urges to hurt or in some way to annihilate me. Play with my father would usually end with more of his rage against me and resulted in a slap across the face or in my head being pushed into the wall. Soon I quit playing games, especially those requiring any physical proximity. Between his invasive touching and outright hits, play was risky at best. Apparently his loss of control was triggered by his own confused feelings of disgust and attraction which yielded to an irrational, explosive violence, as in the day on the tennis court when he used me as a target for his 90-mile-per-hour volley. For more than an hour I took it quietly—for to cry out was to incur even more wrath and more brutality—in the name of "learning to play tennis." It wasn't until I was nearly seventy that I learned that he had done the same thing to his own brother, my uncle, when he was in his twenties. But my uncle was a gifted and talented athlete who returned every volley. On the other hand, I was not. On the way home, my father berated me for being "weak" and a "sissy" because I had black-and-blue marks rising all over my body, and my glasses were shattered. All that I could say to my mother, who was appalled by what she saw, was, "I am learning to play tennis with Dad." It was another shocking moment met with silence. I got the message: Don't complain, don't blame, and above all don't cry.

The years of battering and abuse in this virtual war zone bore with them the scars, ever-deepening silence, and a developing failure on my part to bend to my parents' will for pain or pleasure. I became inured to the pain for the fear of more, and came to welcome the accompanying emptiness and silence. These were all part of the same nightmare. I considered it "normal" when my mother confessed in a drunken stupor, "You should have been the abortion I never had" and "Today I wish you had been aborted!" Even after all the years of abuse, this verbal assault severed my soul like an attacker's blade. I couldn't believe with my head what my heart already knew.

Six years into my marriage, I had a few years of therapy under my belt and the painful discovery that my upbringing was far from normal. I was thirty-three years old, on the verge of becoming a parent of our firstborn, Deborah Michelle, who was wanted, desired, and planned

The tennis player: Bill Karpf on the courts at Depew Park, Peekskill, New York, 1958.

for in every way. While Kaye and I wanted a child by then, I was constantly fearful of my own ability or motives to be an effective parent. I just didn't want to repeat the nightmare of the past, of being an unwanted, unloved child or an ungrateful and unloving parent.

Transformation and Growth

One never recovers from abuse; rather, one learns to transform it from an excuse or a reason for particular behaviors to a means of overcoming or achieving something good. At least, that was my choice and how I chose to use these lessons in terror. My experience became the source of strength. The scars it left, however, led me to resolve that no one could ever get close enough to hurt me like that again. When I allowed it, I usually regretted the outcome, such as with my former partner. Loving meant pain and disappointment, failure and brokenness, or so I always thought—until I learned about and began the spiritual practice of forgiveness.

I had already been well practiced in the liturgical art form of forgiving—that is, announcing forgiveness for all from the altar while maintaining my priestly posture—absolving sins, real or imagined. In the face of sin or guilt, the absolution was among my driving reasons for becoming a priest. Nowhere else in life can one announce forgiveness for others with such authority and presence, yet not necessarily have to live closely or intimately with the offender(s) on a day-to-day basis. Such action clearly has its benefits. It came home to me late in my Gestalt therapy training when I accepted the gift of having a natal chart created by a remarkable mystic and Vedic astrologer from India, Dr. Chakrapani Ullal. From just our first meeting more than 20 years ago, I was thunderstruck at his reading of my life. In that session I even accused him of reading the notes of my therapist and Gestalt instructor, Dr. Rudy Bauer of Washington, D.C. I had just completed five years of deep Gestalt therapy with Rudy in which this territory was well covered. But when Chakrapani explained that, according to my chart, in the House of the Mother there was a vacancy, I couldn't have agreed more as the pain of recognition shot through me. Rather than concede, though, I chose to ask, "What does that mean?"

He went on to explain, "It means that you have had to do this [mothering] yourself—from birthing your life to maturing it—and it is important to remember that you have done this with many women and men over the course of your life and will continue to do so until your death." Then he came to a startling conclusion: "But right now you must learn to forgive your mother. She needs your forgiveness in order to continue her karmic journey. This is not for your sake, but for hers. You must be the father she never knew."

This meant the silence of non-communication for nearly 20 years would now have to end. He was requiring me to break my own self-imposed silence, reaching out to the one who bore me so reluctantly and had exacted such a high price for it. Now I was put into the position of being the one to make peace and heal the breach which I had not created. I was at once overcome and filled with rage and resentment again, and he could tell it.

He quietly continued, "You are the only one who can forgive her and demonstrate what that means in a life. You have the knowledge, the faith, the spirituality, and the sense of rightness to do this. No one else can give her what she needs so completely. And you don't have the rest of your life to do this. It must happen in the next several years. There is little time left." It was 1997.

Breakthrough of Love

My mother had not acknowledged to me that I, her firstborn son, was gay. Now I was being told by an astrologer that I would have to forgive her in order for her journey to continue where it must. It felt like emotional blackmail and something out of the handbook on "how to do a life." I was reluctant to concede any ground on that line and would hold that position for another two years, before events of my life compelled me to do the work. It was the betrayal by my own partner, Buck— the collapse of my most primary relationship in my fifty-second year of life and the loss of my way of life as I knew it—that would force me to move forward with this needed action of forgiving.

In August 2000 I had a highly visible and responsible job as deputy to the bishop of Washington, D.C., responsible for clergy deployment and congregational development and was also one of several canons of Washington National Cathedral. By every professional definition I had arrived. I was stronger than I knew in the face of this particular assault on my life, while my foundation of home and relationship was being destroyed by my own partner. Within six months of his telling me that he wanted a new partner and a new life, I was living in a furnished garage with one of the staff of Church House (the offices of the Episcopal Diocese of Washington, D.C.), and later would rent rooms in an apartment of a close friend. My monthly household income was cut by two-thirds as I went from being prosperous to being functionally broke. My daughter was in her first year at university and my son was getting ready for his sophomore year in high school. Before the end of that unforgettably displacing summer, my boss—Seventh Episcopal Bishop of Washington

Ronald H. Haines—also announced his retirement four months hence, five years earlier than it had been planned, due to the rapidly declining health of his wife, who had Alzheimer's disease. Within four years he would be dead of a brain tumor.

My world suddenly ended as I faced the idea that I would be out of work again as well. It seemed like a good time to consolidate the family trauma and forgive my mother, I thought. All I could do was apologize for the years of silence and invite her to Washington to see my home and glimpse a bit of my lifestyle before it ended. At the same time, she had not seen my children since they were aged six and three, so I invited them as well. Within a day of their departures from Washington after being together—mother and her grandchildren—for two days, I

At a 1999 White House press conference on support for Africa and the fight against HIV/AIDS (left to right): The Very Rev. Nathan Baxter, Dean, Washington National Cathedral; Mr. Jason "J" Clement; the Right Rev. Ronald H. Haines, Fifth Bishop of Washington; Archbishop Emeritus, the Church of Southern Africa, the Most Rev. Desmond Mpilo Tutu; the Rev. Canon Ted Karpf, Diocese of Washington; Ms. Deborah Michelle Karpf, daughter; Mr. Warren W. "Buck" Buckingham III, HRSA, Department of Health and Human Services (official White House photograph).

would leave my home and commence the long journey of grieving and rebuilding a life, but not until I had forgiven my mother.

That nightmarish weekend was a restrained celebration of last things and first priorities. It began the journey of learning to love her. Forgiving was one thing, loving her quite another. There was nothing I could find about her that was lovable. Genetics were not enough. My memories of abuse were thick and scabrous. They required ongoing peeling and removal, which was another therapeutic process of grieving the loss of my relationship. After half a year of emotional outbursts and meltdowns of crying just getting to the threshold of ending our relationship, I was not weepy so much as empty.

With Ron's departure, the ascendancy of the Suffragan Bishop Jane Holmes Dixon in January 2001, and the prospect of a year and half of her as interim bishop with a diocesan search until an election of a new bishop, I knew that I no longer had a place to be, much less go to. Bishop Dixon and I had had a rather contentious relationship for several years before I became canon and deputy to the bishop. The distrust between us then was palpable, but over two years it developed into a respect for our differences, though this was not enough trust to be her deputy. Nor was I willing to serve under her leadership.

On the home front, our friends rallied as best they could. Those in common with Buck were sometimes forced to decide with whom they would stand in our separation. Some did not choose me. I know this because while I never asked them, I never heard from them or saw them again. I only learned a few years ago that he had spread the word that I had abused him physically and had hurt him. When I confronted him about this, he disavowed this story, stating that "nothing could have been further from the truth." To our friends it would only become evident over years of revelations and conversations with those who knew us that Buck's words were not the truth and were not representative of the substance of our relationship. In some cases it took more than 15 years for these friends to tell me of what I had been accused and to confess that they never believed it of me. But they indicated in their own telling that they couldn't help but wonder because his tale was so compelling. Years of his neglect of their mutual relationships and his ongoing opportunism with others ultimately convinced these friends that I was not guilty of such heinous actions.

Forgiving Myself

The harder part of the journey of forgiveness was to learn to forgive myself without becoming righteous about it. Being a cleric allowed a great deal of latitude in amassing a twisted sense of self-righteousness, while maintaining deeply held resentments and anger. "If only…" rang through my words as I struggled to feel whole and holy, and of course I continued to remain silent. I learned to speak of what was really happening in the moment through cognitive therapy, which was simply a way of speaking about what the complementary and alternative therapies had already established. Often I met with these caregivers in two and three appointments per week, undertaking the expense of thousands of dollars in therapy fees, funded by gifts from friends and health insurance coverage. All of this effort taught me how to articulate through the silences the immediacy of the pain of my life, allowing me to be on my feet and function, while hurting deeply. Occasionally I tried to be sexually or physically responsive with another person, only to discover that my heart and body were not ready for such immediacy or intimacy. The ability to be physically intimate with another never really came back. I could no longer trust my lust to be a guide to anything. For nearly two decades, I have not allowed many to come close to me, although I have tried on several occasions to be "in love" with another. In each case, that person loved my soul or mind, but not my body, and did not want to share physical intimacies, which was good to some extent as I was not really physically accessible. I wanted to be in the worst way, but the battle with my silence or fear continues.

At the heart of it, loving myself or even deeming myself lovable has been a lifelong learning activity, which has slowly, very slowly, become manifest in wholeness, strength, and integration of self. I now inhabit a world of respected folk who are close friends and who care for me, welcoming me into their lives and their homes at any time in any way. Life is less manic and I am more grounded than I have ever been, without the added grandiosity or fantasy. When I was in the legal struggle over the home place in New Mexico, I was counseled to accept the cash gifts of friends and allow them to share the problem about which I was deeply ashamed to even be in need, thinking instead that I was stupid and incompetent. A wise counselor simply directed, "Take a dollar bill from your billfold and place it over your heart, repeating these words: 'This is a sign of the love coming toward me.'" Sounds kind of quaint or cute and even a bit simplistic and reductionist. I was instructed to repeat that phrase for each dollar received from my friends, some $30,000 in all! That's a lot of repetition. As of this writing, I am up to about $19,126. I guess it takes a long time to believe that there is that much love for me in the universe.

Anxiety, Death, and Loss

But back to Mother. After our initial encounter in August 2000, our tenuous relationship continued for a while longer until I confronted her with the fact that she had denied my sexual orientation for as long as I could remember. After a great deal of hemming and hawing over the following years, she began to unfold the long-held story of her realization of my sexuality at toddler age and the saga of her self-hatred. She had read that it was the mother's fault if a boy child grew up to be homosexual, which was a belief of psychologists and doctors in the 1940s and 1950s. I was now fifty-seven years old and it was 2005. When I was a child, she explained, she had shared her fears about me and my orientation with my father. After his rage and blame, together they decided that I was to be "toughened up" through physical abuse and beatings. As she was fond of saying, "If you can survive this, you will survive anything!" When I said that it might have been more effective and less costly to us all to try love and acceptance and normalcy, she could only question me, saying, "So what would that have done? Look at you, it must have worked. You have survived everything that life has thrown at you." It was as if the success of my life was her vindication, rather than a testament to my survival instincts and my will. I could only say, "But imagine what my life would have looked like if I had thought I was loved!"

We never talked of this again, for I was challenged to forgive her misguided way of thinking about me, my sexuality, and relationships, and to say so with all my heart. But I felt compelled to add, "Science and research suggest that homosexuality is no more a matter of choice than needing to eat in order to be alive. It seems that while homosexuality may well be genetic, it is more than likely to be inherited from the father's genes."

When I told her this, she wept, saying, "And your father blamed me all those years. Yet he was the one who exclusively sought out male friends. He was the one who didn't even like women." We both let the silence carry the full weight of our thinking and the history of his behavior and loathing toward me to be mutually acknowledged. We never discussed this aspect again. Another silence.... And perhaps another resolution of some kind.

In the months before her death at age 86 in 2011, she asked me to hear her confession as her son, "the priest." She had never previously acknowledged that I was a cleric and that she rather hated the Church. I relented when she insisted and did not want to speak to another priest, and so I went ahead in hearing her confession. Now absolved, she continued to talk of God and judgment. She wound up her argument by saying, "You know, when I die I am going straight to hell for all the painful heartache that I have caused. You of all people probably know it best."

I said, "Actually, I do. But no, you are not going to hell. You are not damned. You will indeed be terrified for just a moment, as many often are, as you review your life and all the missed opportunities ... to love and to have been loved and to accept the love that God gives all of us, unconditionally. Yes, you will be judged, but by yourself."

"Yes," she interrupted, "and that harsh judgment is what I mean by hell and damnation."

Mother. Joan Shepherd Karpf, 2009.

"But, Mother," I interjected, "yes, judged, but by God and found to be … beloved … and then you will fall into the arms of love … and there you will be loved, infinitely and forever, which is what has been here for you all along."

With that she wept but still looked searchingly into my eyes, asking, "And how do you know this?"

"Because," I assured her, "God has told me, Jesus has shown me, and I have spent my entire life being with the dying and living as an advocate for the downtrodden and oppressed. I have seen it thousands of times with my own eyes."

"But can God really love…. Even me?" she pleaded.

"Yes, Mother, even you. After all, I love you. Do you really believe that God being God is weaker than me?" And with that she fell into my loving arms with many deep sobs and grace-filled tears.

"You know, you really can't hear that enough in a lifetime," she said.

"I know, Mother…. You taught me that." With tears of love running down my face, I kissed her cheek for the first time in nearly two decades. She died some months later, but took on a different demeanor and mental attitude in those final months. She was a bit less combative and a bit less fearful. And on the day of her death, she fell into a coma and died quietly…. Falling into the arms of love.

Forgiveness and Love

Forgiveness and love are curiously intertwined, one begetting the other in no particular order, but both necessary to find wholeness and integrity in a life. Both are essential and rarely seem easy if one has been battered, bruised, blighted, or blinded by the tragedies of living. Learning forgiveness and loving are utterly essential to finding a life of value and graciousness. It is not so much a final exam in living as it is an ongoing realization of living and drawing life from the sources of life. It is like entering a room and turning on a light. In the midst of blinding light, at last one's vision becomes clear enough to see the source of light and find comfort in it. Some of us are fortunate to have known such love early on in life and have, as a result, lived fully and richly with forgiveness and grace. Others of us—I am one—are long-term students in the school of grace, still practicing the details of forgiveness and trying desperately to live it. Still others, like my mother, do deny its existence and may have to wait until the final moments of this mortal life to find that such love and forgiveness were there all along. But the undeniable truth of it is that such love is infinite and forever, which allows the process of forgiving to be infinite and forever as well.

Jesus of Nazareth was once asked, "How many times do we forgive?" His answer, which was the multiple of a number equal to the notion of perfection and infinity, was "seventy times seven." I would suggest that is just the beginning.

III

Self-Acceptance and Mentoring

To do for yourself the best that you have it in you to do—to grit your teeth and clench your fist in order to survive the world at its harshest and worst—is, by that very act, to be unable to let something be done for you and in you that is more wonderful still. The trouble with steeling yourself against the harshness of reality is that the same steel that secures your life against being destroyed secures your life also against being opened up and transformed by the holy power that life comes from....

You can survive on your own; you can grow strong on your own; you can prevail on your own; but you cannot become human on your own.
—Frederick Buechner, *The Sacred Journey*

Integrating body and mind and spirit is a crucial part of becoming human and being alive and living with kindness for one another. But it is hard to be spiritual or even intellectual if one is afraid, especially when one is broken physically or emotionally or similarly deeply wounded. I was all of that and more, and seem to have always been fearful (at least inside where no one could see). That's what my mind told me. Fear is that bitter taste on your tongue that never seems to go away, or the tension in your back anticipating something painful like a slap on the face or a punch in the gut; it is the skipped beat of your heart at the sound of someone's anger or a thousand other subtle physical cues signaling that pain and humiliation are near. I remember being fearful of assault or retaliation all the time, either for standing up for something or just ignoring it. The only way for me to get through a physical threat was to

45

act as if it didn't bother me. Drama and tears seemed to provoke more pain and little respect. Silence, whenever possible, seemed to deprive the abuser the reward of my pain. Sometimes, that would backfire and create greater ire, producing more rage and more pain. It was, on a good a day, a crap shoot.

Human Wiring

The environment of my upbringing left me often feeling fearful and inadequate because it had bodily consequences, especially when it came to physical activity. At the time, I did not understand why I hated gym and anything which required coordinated action. As far as I knew, I possessed no eye-hand coordination. Ball and racket sports were simply well beyond my ability. Individual sports like running and swimming were slightly better and actually had the salutary effect of helping me improve my coordination. I have subsequently learned that it was a matter of myelination of the nerves. I had no knowledge of the term until third year in graduate school in a course on developmental education. Myelination is the development of the sheath of insulation (myelin) which protects the nerve and promotes functional, continuous, equal, electrical conductivity within them. When one is not properly exercised in infancy and not effectively stimulated to crawl in order to walk, over time something gets missed—that missing part is the growth of myelin. Net effect on the body is lack of coordination in physical function. There seems to be an interrelated brain dysfunction that accompanies the phenomenon as well. A great rehab technique, for example, for incarcerated persons with behavioral problems is to teach them to crawl and then retrain them on how to walk, through dance and specific exercises. Behavioral and social-conditioning changes for the better are the result of such efforts.

Apart from the psychic challenges of battering, there are the physical debilitations of not being physically developed, thus creating an overt sense of personal failure from the beginning of school through university. It is of little wonder to me that I quickly took on the 1950s cultural characteristics of a "sissy"; that is, a boy who functioned more like a girl. The sense created in me was one of being disembodied. I became effeminate without the necessary movements and subtle behaviors of a real girl. I was in gender dysphoria, for my body was male and my mind was male. I couldn't and didn't want to match up with the female imagery of being sissy. My body failed to protect me, often bringing me pain at the hands of others. Psychically disengaging from it (the body) became a coping strategy and a means of living in the world without being subjected to it. Using my brain and mouth, I became a smartass in insulting peers or even teachers, one of whom it was said had a nervous breakdown after dealing with me in the sixth grade; and I became—what adults termed—a son of a bitch in the way I treated my siblings and friends through verbal or mental abuse, not unlike my forebears. It was a means to getting an upper hand by out-thinking and even outsmarting the world, no matter who it was bearing the brunt of my behavior. I found the secret was to minimize the effect of that trait and, in fact, play at being passive-aggressive, a veritable screwing with a person's mind.

What didn't change was my sense of awe about males who demonstrated their muscular development and physical coordination and any kind of athletic prowess. I often attributed near magical powers to their ability and strength. The attribution of mystical power came as much from my incapacity as from their demonstrated skill. It was a convoluted world of fear and awe. It often led me into disagreements on the professional side through protracted conflicts over minor points of programming or purpose until I learned about power and anger, fear and rage through therapy. So it was not surprising, though deeply challenging, to realize that I needed all kinds of mentoring to complete the needed synthesis of body, mind, and spirit. While the body came last and late in life, the mind and spirit were starving to death. I needed at least one person who would trust me and whom I could trust and then enable me to be me.

The Power of Mentoring

Over time and with a great deal of practice, combined with the willing tutelage of two mentors, through perseverance and loss I eventually found my way to fullness and strength, confidence and courage, competency and generativity through tough love, respect, trust, and accomplishment. One cannot be mentored or even upheld, though, until one is willing to learn. That takes having enough ego to have some sense of one's own values and purpose, yet be unknowing enough to realize that there may be something more to learn. Thus it wasn't until I was a first-year seminarian in graduate theological education at Boston University School of Theology in 1970 that I found the two men who would introduce me to crucial aspects of the fullness of life in its many possibilities, thereby opening the doors to my discovery of the larger world around me. Ever since knowing these two men and being open to their careful and loving tutelage, I have had a series of several gifted guides. Among them were friends and faculty, colleagues and lovers, and indiscriminate parental types who took me in and loved me for myself as one needing their distinctive guidance, compassion, or support. But loving with such complexities and given the ambiguity of many relationships, it was, and in many ways still is, a challenge to grow and change.

Of the first two mentors chosen by me and me by them, most notable was the Rev. Dr. George Litch Knight (1925–1995). We met while I was on a manic Christmas vacation road trip from Boston to Memphis in 1970. George, pastor of Lafayette Avenue Presbyterian Church in Brooklyn, New York, had been the summer employer of my boyfriend at the time, Franklin, who had interned in Brooklyn the previous summer. Franklin was curiously insistent that George and I meet. We did, and from that moment on George couldn't get me out of his mind, nor could I get him out of mine. As a Texan, after a semester of seminary in Boston, I had developed a reputation of being a deeply evangelical and passionate young man. I offered liberal or radical diatribes at the drop of hat. But I possessed a deeply held desire to know and experience as much as possible about everything! It was clear that George, who was two decades older than I, was captivated and intrigued and attracted. A native of Rockford and a member of the Chicago McCormick family (of harvesting company fame) and the Knight family (his father a well-known lawyer and partner of Clarence Darrow), George was a rare hybrid of skilled organist and musician, preacher, and pastor. A founder of the Hymn Society of America and student of nationally acclaimed professor and organist Clarence Dickinson, George was deeply influenced by his relationships to and the teachings of Paul Tillich and Reinhold Niebuhr, applying their theological thinking and social action framework to the application of ministry in the New York Metropolitan area in the late '50s and through the '60s and beyond. Meeting him in 1970 began a bond which lasted to his death in 1995.

From our first encounter he made a probing and extensive inquiry, wanting to know everything about me. At that point, I was so well defended that there was little revealed and a great deal to know, as we both would discover over the following years. Everyone should have at least one total stranger in their life who just gives a damn about who that person is and is willing to extend themselves to find out. George was that gift to me, and to a large extent a gift of God, though I was hardly in the position to reciprocate. I would discover that I was living out a hope he had for me and for the world. I was not alone in this as he often took on a number of "protégés" in a wide variety of professions and callings—music, social work, theology, education, and social change—loving some of us more than others.

His aloofness and shame-filled fear over his own closeted gay sexual orientation sometimes left him helpless in the face of his passions to love or to assist or enable some of us to move on. But I was one of "the chosen"—all the way to his death—as we stayed in constant contact and communication in spite of a family who wanted him to sever all of his relationships to the past, particularly to younger men.

As mentors are wont to do, George directed my life at my behest for several years as I learned the world and the church and the devil through his guidance and support—financial, physical, and psychological—and his demand was that I simply think and act critically and strategically, but always faithfully and in good conscience. It took a period of his careful tutelage for me—for I was still acting like a smartass and distrusted anyone and anything—to learn to be comfortable with him. I believe he would have liked me to be his lover, and I might well have been, but there was a 20-year age gap between us. Despite me believing this gap fine then as well as now, he didn't trust himself and the hostility of the world we lived in. After all, it was only two years after the Stonewall uprising in 1969 and the real beginning of a gay rights consciousness. While I was becoming attuned to the notion of being true to one's own sexuality, George came from a shame-based generation around the matter of sexuality and orientation. Those differences were significant and while I was still in pieces of a person and not really ready for a full-on relationship, I have often thought that it would have been nice to have tried to be his partner.

Nonetheless, George saw me as inherently gifted with a worthy pedigree through my forebears from Boston. While I was one who could be cultured and appreciative of the finer things, that opportunity had been curtailed in my growing up: my family—relatively poor, violent, struggling—provided little to no support, access, or opportunity for appreciation of these things. My mother had come from a background of culture, but my father rarely valued it as inherently useful or good. Any focus on music, and the arts particularly, brought out my gay tendencies, so at home these were not encouraged or desirable traits. George insisted on cultivating my tastes and interests, literally. In every encounter in those first years, he insisted that we have a variety of outstanding culinary experiences to round out my appreciation for and understanding of food, dining, good wines, fine liquors, and the subtlety of their tastes and textures. He challenged me to attend, listen, see, and feel concerts, plays, art exhibits, and public lectures to broaden and enhance my understanding of the world and the interplay of cultures on human beings. As a test, I was expected to report fully on everything I saw and what it meant and why. So I was wined, dined, and feted on the best New York had to offer in the 1970s, with weekly flights subsidized by George to New York City and back to Boston, where I was in school, continuing my formal graduate education at Boston University School of Theology from 1970 to 1974.

Leaving School for the World

But in the fall of 1971, I was overwhelmed with everything in my life and took a leave of absence from school. George recognized my hunger to see the world during this time away and so provided an open airline ticket around the world and the funds to keep me on the road for nine months. During that period, I traveled extensively in the United Kingdom, France, Germany, Switzerland, Italy, Greece, Jordan, Lebanon, Syria, Israel, Egypt, Libya, Tunisia and Spain, visiting churches, temples, holy sites—ancient and modern—meeting fascinating and alluring people, attending theater performances, listening to concerts, engaging in political discussions, living in collective community experiments, and generally surveying the roots of modern civilization. It was all good.

Writing letters of introduction, George introduced me to the world. As a result, I was invited to work in what today would have been called an internship at the World Council of Churches, under the supervision of General

Reporting in the Mass Communications Division is Deacon Ted Karpf, World Council of Churches, Geneva, 1972.

Secretary Eugene Carson Blake and the tutelage of Communications Director C. Michael de Vries. Dr. Blake, who was the former president of the National Council of Churches and an active civil rights leader in the 1950s and 1960s, was a Presbyterian minister and close friend of George. Michael, a senior officer at WCC and protégé of Blake, later became a leader in the Dutch Reformed Church in the Netherlands. He was a remarkable and profoundly effective communicator and theologian. I corresponded with both men until their deaths.

Seeing the world at large was limited only by my imagination: I went to see the architecture and art and to feel the pulse of European capitals as well as cities and communities in North Africa, the Middle East, and Eastern Europe. That season of travel allowed me to be appreciative of the ambiguities now revealed through travel and discovery, of international service and cultural sensitivity, and of awareness to the nuance of languages and respect for things different or even unusual. Travel gave me a distinctive kinship with the world, allowing me to feel at home with people from all over the world, while often attempting to speak to them in their own languages. That initial investment of a Presbyterian minister in 1971 led to an enriching, far-flung, and creative international ministerial career through the Anglican Communion in Africa, and as a public health professional on the world stage through the UN and the World Health Organization, which could have never been possible but for a man who saw a future in me that I could not see in myself at the time. Particularly when I was just learning what it meant to be a human.

After months exploring, I returned to Brooklyn as summer pastor at Lafayette Avenue Presbyterian Church in the summer of 1972 with a world of experiences captured in images, sunrises, and sunsets. My country was a place of wars and rumors of wars as an angry, frustrated, and broken America faced the re-election of Richard M. Nixon as president of the United States, and the war in Vietnam was still underway.

Ted Karpf as summer pastor in June 1972, Lafayette Avenue Presbyterian Church, Fort Greene, Brooklyn, New York.

But I was changed. Having been in the world and among its peoples, I realized that I could not be a small-town provincial boy from Texas anymore and that there was a place for me out there somewhere, even if I didn't know where it was or how I would get there. I also discovered competencies and passions that I still didn't know how to handle, much less control. But most of all I felt myself believed in, supported, and upheld—an incomparable combination. George did all of this, and I remain in his debt forever.

In time I would also come to learn about the variety, range, and flexibilities of my varied sexualities and interests, gently, as I had held myself unusually aloof during the time of my travel and immediately thereafter. But I was now curious about my sexuality and was eager to know more. George held the key to that gate of discovery as well. Demonstrating trust and compassion, he encouraged me firmly, but indirectly, to pursue therapy by sharing with me that he himself was in therapy, and modeled it by sharing tales of some of his therapeutic sojourns and discoveries. It was clear that I was very much myself, albeit still under construction. By mid-term of 1973, I finally started the therapy process, beginning with parsing my world one step at a time. The process of removing the onion-skin layers of my life would continue for decades, but at least I was willing to undergo the process, tearing off all the tacky bits and the cloaking mechanisms to reveal the broken but willing human person.

Commencement, Internship, and Marriage

After the completion of my seminary studies in 1974, I took an internship in Washington, D.C., but would pop up to New York to see George from time to time over that first summer. When I decided in November 1974 to go to the United Kingdom and work full-time in the British Methodist Church for an academic year, George once again supported the work by underwriting my travel expenses. A year later, when I married Kaye Margret Blanche Reynolds of Taunton, Somerset, England, I called George to talk it over as he knew me better than almost anyone. He was supportive of my attempt to marry, on the condition that I had disclosed to Kaye everything there was to know about me and my overall understanding of my sexuality. I had discussed this with Kaye several times. He was concerned nonetheless, but relieved that I was being honest about my own misgivings. Six years later when I determined that I had to live my life and ministry as an Episcopal priest, again I talked it through with him. He asked me to come to New York for several days just to thrash it out and test my thinking and reasoning, as much as my sense of calling. I told him first, before my parents, when Deborah was born in 1982, and again when our son David was born in 1985. I went to see George in 1986 after having what therapists call a "root dream" (a pivotal and often intense dream about coming to terms with the deeper realities of one's life) in the midst of all the AIDS deaths in Dallas. And I told him in detail of my initial chance meeting with Buck before we began a relationship. When I decided to take up life with Buck, I went to George and again talked it through for several days.

What was striking is that he was always there, ready to listen to me and to my process. He tested and pried, pushed and prodded for me to be as forthcoming and honest with myself as possible. Whether he agreed with what I was about to do or not, he always supported me and never dismissed me. In the years that followed, after Buck and I became a household, he would call and talk with either of us, whether I was there or not. George was in every way a mentor, friend, colleague, monitor, and even a father.

Because he was someone who thought I was worthy of the time and the energy he spent on me, lifting me up when I needed it, supporting my voracious curiosity and passion for life, I have become who I am in large part because he helped make me who I am. While much has been made of mentoring, at its heart it is nothing more complicated (or less, for that matter) than the unquenchable belief in another by having the wherewithal and desire to help where and whenever needed, and by being consistently present for that person in all stages and in all conditions.

The Life of Mind and Heart

During this same time, I went through a totally different mentoring approach to life under the tutelage of Dr. Joseph C. Weber. It was September 1970. I hadn't been in Boston for more than a week when the entire entering class, more than 200 of us, went off to a church camp outside of Boston for a class retreat of bonding and orientation. While it was the time of the "winding down" of the war in Vietnam, many were still being drafted and some were dodging the draft at the behest of BU's pacifist dean and ethicist, Dr. Walter G. Muelder.

Being brand new and not living in the school's dormitory because I was living with my great aunt in Quincy to save money, I hadn't yet found anyone with whom I was particularly comfortable. I was very much a loner. We were at a break and invited to go swimming in the nearby lake. I was there quickly: swimming has always been the way that I could physically let off steam or anxiety and at the same time accomplish something. (Some 44 years later I still swim more than a mile every other day.) But on this afternoon at the end of the lazy summer days of 1970, I jumped into the lake and swam out to the floating dock. Sitting on top was a man who appeared to be older than most students, slender and tall with large, wide-open eyes. His name was Joe, he told me, as he extended his hand to help me board the rocking float. After the niceties of "Who are you?" back and forth, to my chagrin he turned out to be among the newer and younger professors teaching systematic theology. He had just arrived two years before from Ecumenical Institute at Bossey, Switzerland, an institution of the World Council of Churches.

He couldn't help but notice that I was cruising him; that is, taking him apart physically, feature by feature. He didn't discourage me. It is often what humans do, I believe, upon meeting an interesting or attractive new person. I was thrilled and titillated to recognize and to be recognized by an adult male who seemed to be seeing me as attractive and worthwhile. Our brief moment ended when he asked me, "Why are you here, Mr. Karpf?" I would come to learn it was his way with students and something he would do to me often. I mumbled something about ministry and service and "becoming a preacher, I guess."

He rapidly responded by saying, "You're here to become a theologian."

My response was one of shock as I was there to become a minister, not a scholar. So I shot back, "No, I'm not!"

That was not enough for him, nor would it ever be. He raised the assault again: "You are here to learn theology and become adept at seeing

The Rev. Dr. Joseph C. Weber, Boston University, 1972.

and hearing the world in this particular way. It is your key and your tool to interpret reality—both that of God and humankind—and you will do theology daily by every word that you say or preach, and every time you open your mouth to speak. Thus, sir, you are here to become a theologian, and I hope a decent one at that!"

I then proceeded to jump off the dock and swim back to shore; he joined me, swimming alongside, still pressing his point and yet beguiling me with his interest. Being a novice at this, I was at once embarrassed and abashed, attracted and aroused, and deeply fearful of everything.

Over dinner Joe pressed his case even further, during which I learned that he was also married with two children. So my prurient interests passed quickly as I found myself defending my chosen direction to go into the work of global mass communication about the Christian faith. He would have none of it, and continued to chide and challenge me for the next two days.

Starting classes on the following Monday, I was deeply relieved that he would not be one of my professors. I simply had no adequate answers in the first weeks of class, nor did I ever for about a year, struggling with the curriculum and demands of scholarship and job. During that time, I took courses in religion and the arts, and ethics and communications at the School for Mass Communications, but would regularly see Joe at chapel services, where he would greet me warmly. He preached occasionally, and I was deeply impressed with his thorough grasp of the preaching material. His style was dry and rather academic but profound in implication. He also taught ecumenical studies and was widely held to be demanding and, at times, unreasonable in his passion and teaching. Was I surprised? No. Every now and then he would come and sit near me in the refectory. Even in those encounters I tended to be either reactive or passive rather than initiating. He finally picked up on it and demanded to know what had happened. Why was I so cool? I usually failed to answer with anything of substance. I was fearful, embarrassed, and confused about his intentions and mine. So it went through the fall term and into the winter term, saying little, offering less.

In the spring he preached a particularly intense sermon for Holy Week. He asked the question, "Do the dead really rise? If so, what is the evidence and the implications for our lives?"

Absolutely provoked, I went up to him afterward and requested time to talk about the sermon. He agreed, and there began the intense relationship of reciprocal academic rigor that I had been seeking and the kindling of the intellectual fires to which I was attracted. I finally admitted to myself that, despite my ongoing emotional distraction and physical attraction, he had things to say that I needed to know. He brought mindful, scrupulous, precise focus to the theological task. He was clearly a man on fire as well as a man of faith. His faith was more radical and more explosive and more upsetting than anything that I had ever seen or heard. But he was not like the professors at Perkins School of Theology at Southern Methodist University in Dallas. Religion students at Texas Wesleyan regularly encountered faculty from SMU at annual conference activities and church meetings. While he was not a classical orthodox theologian, he was fiercely neo-orthodox: his orthodoxy included the work of the contemporary and ancient Greek philosophers and thinkers, as well as French socialists, German communists, American pacifists, and Latin American liberationists. It spoke to crisis and I resonated with it.

Joe was daring and open and very disciplined in his research and teaching, often finding himself engaged in theological rants during seminars, typical of the European scholars of the period. Most of his students were at the doctoral or post-doctoral level. I was a new kid, new to the theological task, so I just sat in and listened, wondering whether I would become adept enough one day to participate. Our collegial student-faculty relationship gave way to a special relationship of deep compassion and love. Joe and later his wife and family loved me and I loved them. He wasn't a peer by age, experience, and academic achievement, but I felt peerage with him emotionally and spiritually. Somehow we wanted the same things in life. This level of engagement provided an entirely different venue from which to see him as my mentor, but from the inside: in his own home place and within his own skin.

Home Away from Home

Because he was in a marriage and had a family, he was less threatening to my psyche than George was. So I jumped into the Weber household, where I was invited into the heart of the family and their lives and would remain there for many years as "Teddy Bear." All the while Joe insisted on maintaining his relentless vigil about my calling and larger purpose. Over the years I would accompany him through a number of personal and family crises. He would question me about my unfolding sexuality as a predominantly gay or bisexual man. His expectation for me was to learn to be as intense and disciplined and demanding for intellectual honesty and substance in all things as he was, especially my sexuality. I succumbed to this aspect of his will completely until it became my own way of life. It has never left me.

Throughout the remainder of my seminary years, I was a constant guest over whole weekends, and often on weekdays for dinner in the evening with the family. A year before my graduation the family moved to Washington, D.C., where Joe had taken up similar duties at Wesley Theological Seminary at American University. Upon graduation I lived with them in Bethesda, Maryland, in the summer of 1974. I was doing an internship with the American Association of Retired Persons (AARP) in religion and public relations. Later that year, I returned to Europe for work in the British Methodist Church as a supply clergy and full-time chaplain at the City of Bath Technical College and Bath University, where I met Kaye. But I remained in continuing contact with Joe and the family. Shortly after Kaye and I married, his son Robert lived with us, working on nearby farms and ranches during a gap year after high school. Kaye and I visited with the Weber family when we made our first trip in 1977 to a family wedding in New England. I would see them when I attended courses at the College of Preachers at the Washington National Cathedral. Our deep and soulful conversations and visits continued for the next decade.

Few people could have held me so enthralled with theology and intellectual rigor. Even as he was dying in early 1986, some 15 years after our first meeting, he still held the same scrupulous concern over me. As I responded to the crisis of his illness, he would often ask me if I understood what was happening to him. I would have to say, "No, I don't understand what's happening to you, but because of what is happening in my parish with all these AIDS deaths, I do feel the pain of loss and the fearsomeness of dying all around me." Then he would ask me if I feared death. I would say, "I do not fear death." I was already experiencing the onslaught in my own parish of the deaths of dozens of young men. "But," I admitted, "I cannot bear the loss of you from my life. You have had such profound impact on me, my ministry, and my understanding of wholeness and acceptance. Above all I will love you always." We both cried and held one another as our last farewell ended. Our next encounter was at the columbarium fountain in Bethesda, where he was interred. I have visited there often just to talk to him about the work, my life, and the challenges of my faith in the decades that followed, especially during my Diocese of Washington years in the 1990s through 2004.

We Never Do This Alone

These two men—both clergy, both thoughtful, needy, and deeply introspective, both demanding in their own ways, particularly within the disciplines they practiced—loved and cared and supported me through the awkwardness of my own post-adolescent psychological, spiritual, intellectual, and theological development. But more than this, as mentors George and Joe treated me as a peer and partner, colleague and comrade, friend, and confidant, and often became my personal promoters. I have never known such trust and devotion from two such men who were at once my elders, my advocates, and my friends. Over the course of years, even as their lights faded, they have remained ever-burning presences in my life: calling me out, calling me to account, and demanding that I bring my best—body, mind, and spirit—into any situation. They demonstrated and demanded integrity and clarity, even when I was unsure of my willingness or ability to offer such. They continue to beckon me not only onward, but upward. As the mentors they were, today they remain my spiritual/soul guides and comforters for a lifetime that seems, at times, all too short. I have always wanted to have such an impact on other lives as they have had on mine, and I have attempted to make it so with several mentees while I complete my journey. Like them, I have not been disappointed with this role of mentoring.

These men modeled courage and perseverance to me, and in turn I was able to embrace the demands they made and model them to the world. They challenged me repeatedly to live into the fullness of my own being and urged me to reach beyond my own deeply held barriers and fear of responsibility and commitment. They assured me that I was indeed loved and accepted, but that life demanded more of us than the burden and opportunity for love. Both insisted that I use my mind to the fullest and not fall into lethargy or laziness. And finally, both created a sense in me that faithfulness over the long haul, especially when one does not anticipate or even understand the potential outcomes, is faithfulness for life. These men helped me see that the main calling in this life is prayer forward for another generation of men and women. They inspired me to acts of sponsorship and support for a number of ecclesial leaders as well as artists, musicians, poets, and writers. They taught me how to follow my heart when supporting another and to love them and my own offspring, unconditionally, even when it hurt to do so.

Passing the Gift On

To honor what was given to me, mentoring has become a fact of my daily life as priest, professional, father, and friend. Always aware of their untapped talent, hidden skills, courageous vision, and crystalline sense of calling, several dozen folk have been beneficiaries of the gifts engendered in me by my mentors. There are now more than a half dozen clergy serving in parish communities across the country, along with administrators of charitable institutions, public health and other health professionals, social work leaders, and public servants around the world who have come to me to more clearly understand or discern their responsibilities and opportunities in answering a call to give of themselves in service to others. Often serving as mentor or guide to these committed human beings is both privilege and obligation. It is privilege because it constitutes some sort of payback to those who believed in me so long ago and obligation because ensuring the next generation of thought leaders and change makers is on a path toward wholeness gives me a sense that the future, while unknown, is in secure hands, being led by the most capable and compassionate people I have had the chance to know.

Mentorship is about guarding my own needs and listening deeply and attentively to the needs of another, offering respect and concern when and wherever possible. It has been a good experience and model to follow through the whole of my life. And while my affections can run wild and my fantasies go well beyond the bounds, I have not extended myself in such a manner with any whom I have guided or supported. Mentorship then is about falling in love with the future, abiding well in the present, and helping to reveal the past so that a life can be lived to the full.

IV

Identity and Kindness

God is hiding in the world. Our task is to let the Divine emerge from our deeds.
—Abraham Joshua Heschel, *I Asked for Wonder: A Spiritual Anthology*

As you have already learned, I am a gay man and always have been; it is one unmistakable part of my identity. I am a priest in no matter what guise I cover myself. Nonetheless, who I am and what I value have remained constantly questioned internally, while changing in their outward expression throughout my life. There is no doubt that I will continue to change, for that is what it means to be an alive human, but my core—identity and values—remains the same. Even with the changes that are real, especially as experienced in aging, accommodating to limitations and diminishment, I have been able to stay awake about life, stay current in a world of changes, and continue to enjoy the challenges of being consistent and whole. I tend to think of my ways of being as incarnations: ways of being enfleshed, embodied, or present in the world. I have also carried a number of professional titles: canon, priest, pastor, presbyter, liturgical leader, deacon, elder, missionary, lay person, staff person, federal official, administrator, and diplomat. On the other hand, I am a grandfather and a father to a few; a brother and a colleague, a mentor and a friend, as well as a confidant, confessor, and therapist to many. It all seems quite rational to me. Some may read this as a dodge. Therefore I will weigh in on the notion of identity. It is important to have a sense of self and a notion of personhood to be present in the world as a conscious, deciding, autonomous, cognizant being. For me, the core of self has been and will always remain that I am at once a gay man who is a father and a son. But I am a number of other things as well.

After I had been in South Africa for a little more than a year, Archbishop-emeritus Desmond Tutu asked me how I liked being in Africa. We were busily preparing for the 7 a.m. Friday celebration of the Holy Eucharist at Cape Town's St. George's Cathedral, where it had been his tradition to celebrate for several decades. I was there to help. I looked at him carefully and said, "I'm not sure why, Your Grace, but I feel really at home here. The culture and languages, the environment and people are still alien to me in most respects, but just the same, I feel at home."

Desmond broke into his characteristic giggle that yields to laughter and replied, "Of course you feel at home, Teddy! You were born here." I was about to protest that he might have me confused with someone else, but he went on. "After all, Africa is where all of humanity began. You have merely come home now."

We looked at one another and laughed together, and then I stopped laughing and rejoined, "But I am here now to be sure that humanity does not end here." Moments later we stood at a common table, celebrating the mass in the midst of an HIV/AIDS pandemic ravaging Africa, particularly South Africa, a ministry to which the Anglican Church of Southern Africa had charged me to develop a coordinated response. "Now, I'm here." That affirmation is pretty much how I have come to terms with problems internally as well as with a lifetime of living in alien, albeit wonderful places. It is how I have come to understand the lives of people. Wherever I have lived—from residing in a former bawdy house on a side street in Chemin des Vergers in Ferney-Voltaire, France, to a home named Millstone Lodge, constructed from bits and pieces of some of the great homes in Cape Town, in Noordhoek, South Africa— I have found a way to be at home. Today, I reside on Plaza Blanca, in an adobe look-alike in Santa Fe, New Mexico, next to a very large Arizona cypress whose branches overshadow the roof of my home. But a few years before that I was winding up nearly a year in a 125-year-old Victorian townhouse in the old silk-stocking district of Elmwood in Buffalo, New York.

Being at home wherever I am is both a preoccupation and vocation. So Desmond's words were helpful for me to come to terms with figuring out Africa and, in some respects, my life. I am a child of the world, a citizen of the planet, a human of the earth. Even though it was not spoken, I knew by whatever internal means I had—culture, family, tradition, or experience—that what I was feeling and those to whom I was attracted were clearly wrong to many or not admitted out in the open in the world of the 1950s; otherwise, someone would have talked about it. Fortunately, they do talk about it today. This knowing/unknowing milieu was my first moment of learning in the art of compromising/conforming with and to the culture, my family, the church, and the community at large. The proverbial closet door slammed shut to the notion of honesty when it came to my identity as being gay. Beginning in my pre-adolescent years and continuing until I was in college, I couldn't figure out how I could relate to girls and women, but had a deep sense of attraction and fascination with men. There was an explicit moment, preceded by a lifetime of implicit moments which clearly began much earlier, maybe as much as a decade before adolescence, when I was too young to know what feeling such things meant or why. But I knew in ways that lay beyond me.

It began with my feeling "different" without any particular reference to sexuality. My parents would cast an eye toward me at the oddest moments and just look at me strangely for what I believed was no particular reason. My father was particularly annoyed by my ways of fighting and defending myself. My means of expression through music and the arts, particularly dramatics, and my constant obsession with the Church brought abuse and verbal assaults. As I learned later, they were indeed watching and assessing everything that I did from my earliest age. They tried to mold me, to correct me, so I would turn into something other than what I was or change how I was acting at the moment. It was very confusing.

In my mother's last years, I talked to her about this. She explained my birth and her reasons for raising me this way: "Around the time you were two, I read in a magazine that by the time a child is two years old, sexual identity is set. Your father and I knew that you were a queer ... that is ... a ... ahem ... a ... homosexual. So we took what steps we could, particularly as you approached puberty—from physical correctives and beatings to screaming and correcting you at every opportunity—to get your attention: that you were not like other boys and you

were not to like them either. By insist-
ing that there was a right way to
walk—you know, with a kind of swag-
ger—and how to stand or sit or talk
properly so no one would think that
you were who you were, both then
and now."

I protested, "But you never said
a word. You never indicated that you
knew I was different."

"No," she said, "We never discussed your sexuality with you so you
wouldn't want to be like one of them.
You of all people didn't need to know
that we knew anything and what you
were actually about. When you suddenly surprised us at age 27 by getting married, we thought we had

Ted Karpf, age 4, 1952.

actually succeeded. Now I understand that you had tried to fit in and
really couldn't. Clearly, it didn't last long enough to get you through
a whole lifetime without detection. Though I still think that the 'AIDS
thing' and your work in it diverted you and put you in contact with
those kind of people again and again. What a shame. It destroyed your
life."

I couldn't speak. I was outraged and shocked that my own life had
been kept from me by, of all people, my mother. I was furious that I had
spent decades in therapy on my own nickel trying to make sense of a
life from which my own parents had kept me. I was hurt that love meant
withholding love and trust in order to "steel" me to the rigors of society
and the world.

I finally said, "You know what I have learned from raising two children? That by loving them one can at least give them the assurance that
no matter what happens and who they are, they can always come home.
Seems to me that loving a child provides them more flexibility and ability
to deal with change and contradiction than does brutality."

"At least with us," she said with a tremor in her voice, "we knew that
if you could survive us—your home—you could survive anything."

The Crisis of AIDS and Identity

In a convoluted way my mother was right in thinking the "AIDS thing" had something to do with my eventual coming out. It all came to the fore one evening in 1985, already more than a year into my AIDS work out of the Episcopal Church of St. Thomas in Dallas. I was making a pastoral visit to Wayne, a dying member of the parish, and his partner, John, at their home. I asked John what was the one thing he wanted before Wayne's death. He said, "Ted, I just want to hear from him, just once, that he loved me more than all the boys that he had before me."

Wayne had long ago told me that there were "many boys in my life but none like John, who truly loved me," so this request from his partner and lover of several years, during the descent into illness and death from AIDS, was not only legitimate but heartrending. For reasons that I will never fully comprehend, Wayne suddenly awakened from his coma, wanting to converse with me about his faith and receive Holy Communion one more time before he died. We did all of that. In his tears and fearfulness, the raw exposed feelings of his dying and the unknown of what was to follow called into question my reluctance at mentioning John's final wish for Wayne.

I proceeded to say, "Wayne, John has one question for you tonight before this journey can be properly completed."

He smiled and turned to John and said, "Come on, baby, what's your question? What could you possibly want to know from me at this point?"

John hesitated. I urged him to go on. He did, tears running down his face like a waterfall. "Wayne," he choked up again, now fearful of the answer, "I need to know just one thing.... Did you love me more than all the other boys?"

Wayne just looked at him quietly and longingly, almost shocked, then broke into a warm smile. "Oh, baby, how can you ask that? I have always loved you more than anyone I have ever known. I always knew that ours was the real thing. You are the best one ever. I am so glad and grateful that you are in my life, especially now." With that they embraced and kissed one another as lovers do at airports and on cruise ship docks when heading to separate destinations. Then Wayne lay back and in a few moments returned to the unconscious state from which he never again emerged. God's will had been done in that moment. John wept bitterly for the coming death he was facing. His lover was leaving him, but he was now deeply secure in the knowledge that he was loved by Wayne. We talked about Wayne for a while, and what would happen, no doubt sooner than later. He decided that they should spend this last night together. So I tucked him into bed with his dying lover and promptly left. Wayne died the next day. John would die a year later.

As I headed home, the lights of downtown Dallas ahead of me, I felt my face suddenly drenched in tears, as wet as an immersed, newly baptized infant, sobbing uncontrollably in what soon became a haunting wail that I can still hear today. I kept repeating, "I will never know that kind of love." Between sobs I said to myself, aloud, "I will never have a man who loves me that much. I can never be that honest with anyone. I am so tired of assuring others of God's love for them, but never having any left for me."

For the first time ever, I felt the chasm of deep loss for a life clearly missed and an even deeper vexation at the seemingly hopeless condition of my life. As best I could tell, I was living lies and wanting something totally different! Indeed, St. Thomas parish had exposed me to beautiful, well-adjusted, gifted men: single and gay; partnered and gay; widowed and gay; old, partnered, and gay men. When I arrived home, trying to collect myself, Kaye just looked at me as if she knew

Kaye Margaret Reynolds and Ted Karpf just before the birth of Deborah Michelle, Denton, Texas, February 1982.

what I had been struggling with and how I had fared. I could not cover the tracks of my tears and my very red eyes. I tried to explain what had just happened and then she too burst into tears, confessing that she had felt the same way about me and my attempts to be something that I was not. With brutal honesty she also documented my obvious physical disinterest with her and with my life, especially for the past year. We lived in the liminal space of unknowing and continued to play at being a couple, enacting our public personas for a very long time thereafter. But now we both knew that we were not hiding from it or from one another. We bore our honesty with dignity and respect, but nothing was resolved.

Finally, while on vacation the next year (1986), I was given the gift of a moment of hope for change. Kaye and I were in the U.K. and would depart soon for Paris aboard the Orient Express from London. We were assured that the kids would be well cared for by their grandparents in England while we toured Paris, Bruges, and Amsterdam. Seven days of traveling, just the two of us together, and then some days with her family in Taunton, Somerset, before I returned to Dallas alone. Kaye would have another several weeks or so at home with her family and extended family—a total of a month in the U.K. She was ready and needful for the familiar of being with her family, and I was ready to be alone.

The Root Dream

On our second day back with her family, I became sickly and agitated so I retired and took a long late-afternoon nap before dinner at 9 p.m. Sunset wasn't until nearly 11 p.m. in the U.K. in midsummer. I fell into a trance-like sleep and had a dream. I was no longer in Somerset; I was simply somewhere else, outside but within space and time. First it was half-light, then suddenly there was bright light all around me. I could not make out any of the details of the landscape or place. I didn't know whether I was inside a building or outside. There was a faint scent of something pleasant in the air but I couldn't tell whether it was spices, flowers, the sea, or just a fresh mountain breeze. But it left me feeling clear, open, and secure. The light was reassuring and not threatening. Then I heard a voice speaking to me. Again, I wasn't sure whether I was hearing it or feeling it, or perhaps both. It said, "So here you are. I want you to see your life." I was watching my life roll before me in segments: birth to 5 years old, 6 to 10 years old, 11 to 16 years, and so forth in four- or five-year segments to my then current age of 37.

I was asked after each segment, "Do you have any regrets?" Over and over again, I saw the cause and effects of my life and the outcomes after therapy, to which I always stated, "I have no regrets." And so it continued until my sudden death at 37.

Then I stopped the action and insisted, "I have many regrets right here. I don't know how this story comes out with my children. What happens to them? What do they do? How do they live? I want to know what happens."

So I was shown their lives without me, and it proceeded again in segments, less clear this time, but always the same question: "Do you have any regrets?" To which I always responded, "Yes, I don't get to know how their stories come out and what happens to Kaye, who has obviously re-married." So the journeys and the dream continued with my protest-ing each time until my children reached old age, and then I began to laugh and sob all at once. "I guess the tragedy of life," I said, "is that we will never know the outcome of the next generation. We must just trust that they will be all right."

The movie or screen vanished and was replaced by twilight. I felt the warmth and security of the wisdom that had been shared. I knew in that moment that I had witnessed my death and judgment. I was no longer fearful of dying or dreading the possibility of living and change. There was a great sense of assurance and relief, and there were tears. This time they were tears of joy and release. Gradually I came awake, still sobbing and bathed in the twilight of a Somerset evening.

As I lay there recounting to myself what had just happened, I real-ized that I had been asleep for several hours. I revisited each aspect of the experience, wishing not to forget about my regrets. I realized that I had literally dreamed my death and my *own* judgment, rather than God's, of my life. I judged my life through the lens of regret. This dream was no accident. It was not merely about my children and their futures; but it was more conclusively about my future and self-acceptance. I was thunderstruck by the lack of condemnation, for I had previously held that God is a God of judgment and in that light there was nothing I could do or be which would not be judged, especially the deepest fears of the heart, like being gay. I was terribly wrong when I discovered in that dream that God's judgment was based on my own sense of personal regret.

Therapists call this a "root dream." This dream was about coming to terms with the realities of my life: my sexuality and the fundamental nature of my commitments. I told Kaye about it a few days later, and she agreed that it was, indeed, time to own up to my life. She knew better than I the degree of my internal brooding and discontent. When we parted, with her remaining in the U.K. and me returning home, it was strangely bittersweet. I had no intentions about anyone per se, just that my life would have to change dramatically. As I was leaving, Kaye said, "Do what you need and be ready to welcome us home in a fortnight." The homecoming would not be what I thought I would actually be about and it wasn't necessarily based on anything that I wanted.

Falling in Love

I was home two days and back in the pulpit when someone acquainted with the parish invited me to dinner. His name was Buck, and he was very much the center of everyone's attention as the writer of the first major private foundation grant that would launch the AIDS services program in Dallas: AIDS Arms Network. We returned from dinner out and stopped by his house for a few hours to talk about the grant program and his faith. Just before we finished he asked me point-blank, "Are you gay?" I said, "Yes." For the next 12 days we met up and made love every day—morning, noon, and night—and confessed our undying but exceedingly complicated love and passion.

He had had a partner for several years and explained that they were ending that relationship. I had a wife and children. He began writing to me daily, a routine that lasted nearly two years into our relationship. Kaye returned with the kids two weeks later. When she saw me upon stepping into the arrivals lounge, tears appeared on her cheeks. She leaned into me, whispering, "Who is he?" I put up a vociferous but brief protest, finally relenting and confessing exactly the who, what, and where, all before we arrived at our home 40 minutes later. For a while after that it was challenging and difficult for all of us, but over time she came to know Buck well and learned to love him. But that, too, was problematic.

He and Kaye would go to dinner or he would babysit when Kaye and I would go out. A year later, I attempted to live in an equal relationship with each of them, but the emotional conflict and confusion didn't enhance anything, making life utterly impossible. Finally, Buck and I broke it off in spring 1988, amidst all of our accommodations and my clear reluctance to break with the family. Two years of trying to make all of these relationships work was altogether chaotic and often impossibly demanding. I never seemed to please anyone, least of all myself. He went off to therapy, and I resigned myself to die unhappy. I even considered suicide for a time. Then after two months of virtually no contact, he invited me to meet with him and his counselor, who spent the session challenging me.

After the session, Buck reiterated the challenge in his own colorful language. "Well, it's who you are and you can't avoid it…. You're gay and those are the facts. You enjoy gay sex way too much to be a mere voyeur in this world. There's nothing in you that is straight. So make up your mind. Are we together for the long haul or not?" It was hard to hear this, but it basically was true about me. He seemed to be offering an ultimatum, and I was in the mood to accept his terms. After all, I was about to turn 40. I was seen by many to be a rising cleric in the Church and was still reluctant to let go of the fantasy of my life. Considering his challenge and my emotional state, I decided to make the transition to become "us." After we agreed to get together to make a life, he, Kaye, and I created a plan for a one-year sabbatical 18 months hence, from which I would not return and during which Kaye and I would separate and divorce. All of us would relocate away from Dallas. Then I would be able to begin a new "out" life with Buck. It was all perfect. Too perfect to be real. It is said that "God is what is happening when you are busy making plans."

About ten weeks after this decision, Kaye, the kids, and I were spending time in Telluride, Colorado. It was August 1988 when we received a phone call from Buck. After a long silence he said, "I have momentous news for you, and for us…. All of us: you and Kaye, especially. I must have AIDS. I was diagnosed today with an opportunistic infection. It is evident that I am HIV-positive, but just got tested. I am very ill. Can you come home? I need you."

I can still see that moment. On television was Texas Governor Ann Richards, speaking at the 1988 Democratic National Convention. Just moments earlier, David, then three years old, had fallen into the hot tub on the patio and was crying more from the surprise of it than from fear. The call had come just as we were beginning to unwind this startling surprise with David. Within a few moments, Kaye looked at me and immediately started packing. I was in shock. My whole life passed in front of me as I realized that I would have to resign my position, give up the family, and start a different life.

We left several hours later for the grueling 22-hour drive back to Dallas. Kaye and I talked quietly whenever we could as the kids reflected our anxiousness and frustration. We discussed the practicalities as to how to handle the next 24 hours and next days. The requisite HIV testing for both of us, "outing" ourselves with our doctor, who was also a family friend. We talked about finances and the longer-term implications of my resignation. On arrival in Dallas, exhausted, I put the family in a hotel, where we would remain for the rest of our vacation, because the parish presumed we were in Colorado.

I then went to Buck. All we could do was cry and hold each other. It was clear to me that life would not be what we had planned. The grand plan would not be implemented. It was well-known by laity and clergy alike that the bishop of Dallas, Donis Dean Patterson, was very clear about his lack of acceptance of gay and lesbian people, despite his willingness to confirm them as members of the Church. But for gay/lesbian clergy there was no acceptance—zero tolerance—especially if one was very public about it. There were a few who were so well-hidden that they functioned until recently in that diocese. So looking to the Church or diocese for support or employment was, at very best, very limited. I would learn nearly a year later just how difficult it would be.

Three weeks later I gave notice to the Vestry that I would resign on September 18, my 40th birthday. Buck and I would officially take up life together on October 1. Kaye would remain in the rectory until March 1989, then would relocate outside of Dallas to Richardson and a school district with a built-in pre-school for David. David was three years old and Deborah six. Kaye and I then arranged to meet with the bishop to inform him that we were leaving the parish and that we would be divorcing within the year for irreconcilable differences. In that meeting Kaye said to him, without being sexually specific, "Ted can no longer be the husband I need him to be." The bishop nodded, believing he was understanding without actually understanding any of it. It would be several months later, nearly a year after I was summoned to visit with the presiding bishop, that I would have to tell the same bishop of Dallas what Kaye meant by her words: that I was a gay man and that this is why the divorce was happening. By then, he was outraged and determined to excommunicate me for being gay, as he had learned it from other clergy and the Dallas-area media over the preceding year.

Kaye and I believed that we had done all that we could to make this transition without scandal or public embarrassment. It was hard on both of us already, and a rumor in the Dallas gay media suggested that I was leaving because I was having "an affair" with a local gay man, which was not necessarily untrue, but rather untimely in this kind of public disclosure.

"Outing," as it was called in those days, was the way the more militant side of the gay community could publicly shame detractors of the gay community into politically responsible positions. But since I was neither a detractor nor publicly shaming gay and lesbian people, shaming me in public created a mild backlash among the politically elite of Dallas, allowing Buck and me to continue to hold positions of responsibility in the larger civic community.

To complete our marriage, Kaye and I revisited San Antonio, the site of our honeymoon, acknowledging our thirteenth and last anniversary. That journey to San Antonio was just three days after leaving the parish. It was a bittersweet time in which we called to mind both our best moments and our most difficult ones over those 13 years. We revisited all the places from our honeymoon days, being reminded of our hopes and dreams. We talked openly of the changes and what they would mean to both of us. We agreed that we would both remain actively engaged parents to our children and would find a way to be co-parents. It was a time characterized by deep grief and very real pain over the losses that would be incurred by our separation and divorce and the combination of joy and sorrow about our separate expectations. It was a painful yet fond farewell for both of us, being reminded of what we had started and what good there had been between us, particularly with the gift of our children.

Kaye and I learned—thankfully—that we were both HIV negative. The virus had not been transmitted. I learned in 1994 as part of a discordant partner's study at National Institutes of Health that I had, in fact, been infected, but for reasons that no one can explain, I have never seroconverted to being HIV positive. Each of us also had to face the real possibility that Buck would be dead within a year or two at the outside, because at this time there was little treatment available that really worked. We didn't know what that meant for me and for Kaye and for the children and for the future. Unfortunately we knew from our working lives that no one diagnosed this far down the road would survive.

Then our years together—Kaye's and mine—ended. I moved out of the house and into the apartment where Buck now lived. He had broken up with his partner 11 months before. I packed up my office in boxes on the weekend of my resignation, moving it all into his study at home. For months they remained exactly where I dumped them.

Several weeks later, now unemployed and no longer a functioning priest, I rose late for the first time in decades one Sunday morning. Buck and I drank mimosas and read *The New York Times*; a fantasy I had long held. What I will always remember of that time was waking up next to him that very first morning, thinking, "Ah, this is what it's all about. Waking up next to your lover and partner and feeling complete and whole." For the rest of my life, I would repeat over and over: "At last, I am who I am. No more, no less." That was three decades ago. I am glad that I chose to make a new life, though the cost was—admittedly—very high.

A year later, Kaye and I divorced in family court in Dallas. She had a lawyer who decided to play the "gay card." We lived in Texas, where the law was punitive toward gay folk. The cost of appeal was exceedingly high in terms of time and legal defense. This meant that the settlement was unusually punitive: one half my monthly income; limits to my exposure to the children (though Kaye and I worked out another unwritten agreement); and it was clear that I would never be recognized as a co-parent under any circumstances. I couldn't believe that I was being cast by the lawyer as a perpetrator for just being me, and at the same time I was becoming a victim along with Kaye in this nightmarish proceeding. I entered the courthouse enraged with the whole process and particularly with being cast in such negative light. Nonetheless, I accepted the terms to make us both "honest" in our lives and to give Kaye the freedom to pursue a life as well. Ten weeks before the settlement, though, Kaye co-signed a mortgage for Buck and me when we bought a townhouse in Dallas, our first home.

At our divorce hearing, the judge turned out to be a sympathetic friend of ours. As we stood before him, he asked, "How did this happen? What does it mean?" At that moment, Kaye said something I have never forgotten: "What's happening does not change the fact that I love him, Your Honor, and he loves me. Then it is all that I can do to ensure that he becomes all that he is and all that he can be. If that means ending our marriage, then I am for it." I only nodded in silent assent. Inside, my gut was churning as I felt worse about what was happening, rather than relieved. I reviewed again and again all that Kaye and I had shared about the meaning of love, about my open admission before we were married that I was gay or maybe bisexual, and that I had no desire to hurt anyone. I understood the meaning of abandonment in relationship and now I was inflicting this on Kaye, and yet I clung to the notion that I could at last become myself. The judge sat open-mouthed, then granted us the divorce. We were no longer married.

Our children have since asked each of us on multiple occasions how we could have done this and what it meant. We have struggled to tell them the best that we can without tarnishing the other. It was increasingly evident to me, though, that Kaye and I wanted different things in life that had nothing to do with sexuality, mine or hers. We wanted lives with different endings. We were not different from many couples who, after many years together, have become decidedly different people in what each wanted for a life and how each wanted to live, maturing through our knowledge of the other. We came out of our process with distinctly different visions borne by experience. Without that shared vision for a common future, no matter what happened between Kaye and me, we had little else to build on. That was enough to say.

The kids, now adults, long recognized these differences and have come to see them as part of their own strengths. Kaye, for her part, insisted that her four sisters, mother, father, and other relatives not judge or bad-mouth me: I was, after all, the father of our children, and thus connected to their grandchildren, their niece and nephew, and their cousins. To this day, no one in the family has belittled me to either of our children. For that I am exceedingly grateful. Kaye remarried after several years and became a Mormon: a member of the Church of Jesus Christ of Latter-day Saints. She raised both children in her own home, and together we did the best that we could to meet their needs and support their life concerns. Today we are grandparents, each of us doing what we do best with our granddaughter.

Coming Out: A Repeating Discovery

As for the question of identities or identity, "coming out" as a gay man has continued constantly. When the local gay press "outed" me and the fact of my relationship with Buck, about a year before I was ready to publicly announce my identity, I was without words, not knowing what this all meant yet. I was still trying to protect my career as a priest and actually thought I would be able to do so. After being outed, though, the conflict with the bishop erupted, pretty much ending my career as a rector or parish priest for some years. I was shunned and often silenced when I was suddenly rejected by long-time friends and colleagues dating back to college years and by those I'd developed up to the time of my revelation of sexuality and orientation. I was also accepted by some folks from those years. It was surprising that some people of my parents' generation and ages tended to reject me outright. To many of them, I was an embarrassment and considered as shameful and selfish, obviously denying my family. To them I was dead. My parents, who had heard through Kaye's mother what I had done and what it meant, proceeded to take me to court to assert their rights as grandparents. In my defense, I simply told the court what had happened between my father and me and his verbal abuse in front of my family. I also told of my fear of the risk of my mother endangering my children, based on her past with me. I said nothing in my defense as a gay man. The court ruled in my favor, and the case never came up again. My mother didn't see my children for more than a decade and a half. I recently found the letters she had written to the children on their birthdays and at Christmas and Easter. In them she wishes them well, acknowledging the import of the occasion, and then goes on a rant about how terrible her son was for depriving her access to them. That was then.

After 2000 and for the remainder of her life over the next decade, she had access to them and they to her. As young adults they could no longer be endangered by her carelessness and venom. However, since her death I learned that many relatives were simply told that I was dead or missing. I only learned of this when I decided to spend the past several years reconnecting with long-lost cousins, aunts, and uncles. I have managed to establish an identity as a legitimate family member, albeit the gay one. There has been gentle acceptance and a fair amount of off-the-cuff comments about my gayness from time to time. But by and large, I am back in the family well before the end of my life.

Finding My Jewish Roots

The way people in my father's family handled most conflicts was to consign others to silence or separation, sometimes forever. This was inelegantly depicted when I discovered the graves of my long-departed paternal grandparents in Peekskill, New York. What I saw was a literal separation of my gentile grandmother and Jewish grandfather into resting places apart from others, and in separate cemeteries. I was ashamed of the not-so-subtle discrimination between Christians and Jews, as well as among them. Their marriage is commemorated by eternal separation in death, and further reinforced within the separate communities, where the gentile is interred on a hillside apart from the other Christians of her own family, and the Jew lies resting by a gate at the farthest point from his

Exiled to the farthest point in the Hebrew Cemetery in Cortland, New York, and the farthest point from his family's grave sites sits the gravestone marker for my grandfather, William Karpf, Sr., a veteran of World War I.

Mother (Joan), me, and Grandfather William Karpf, Sr., 1948.

family, down the hill and nearly out of the Jewish cemetery. Perhaps of equal shock was the fact that my uncle—my father's brother and my grandfather's only surviving son—did not go to the cemetery often or tend his father's grave, though he had tended his grandfather's grave as a young man. No one had mentioned any of this to me as a child, and while I had vaguely known my father's father was a Jew and his mother a gentile, the silence around this matter was complete and nearly eternal.

After seeing my grandfather's family plots, I little wondered that my father could banish me forever and I him. It seems that he and I were born to it. Nonetheless, I found myself weeping at the brokenness found in both camps—Christian and Jew—and wondering if tradition is still so divisive today. My aunt and uncle indicated that my uncle would prefer to be scattered on the plots of both to bring them together at last! Finally there was someone who could end the separation and, perhaps in the midst of heartbreak, create a resolution of wonder.

Redemption and Reclamation

Standing at my grandfather's grave at last, I was reminded of the time in 1972, nearly two decades after his death in 1953, that this was the same grandfather—the Jew—who had taught me to pray. I recovered the memory of when I was very small and he took me to the Saturday morning gathering of men in the synagogue called *schul.* I discovered this fact of my life when I attended a Shabbat morning service conducted by a rabbi friend from seminary. It was the first time as an adult that I had entered a synagogue. I found myself spontaneously praying and speaking in Hebrew, which I had never studied. It was Yom Kippur— the Day of Atonement. The ancient Hebrew words of Morning Prayer tumbled out of my mouth and from a place I never consciously knew until that day. It still remains a singular wonder to me to be a Christian priest who began his journey of faith as a small boy praying in the language of Jesus and finding his identity in an expanded tradition of faith as an adult.

I am still gay in my head and heart. I have reached an age where I can comfortably appear as an out gay man in the public biographies of gay and lesbian religious leaders, and in other references on internet biographical resources without fear of reproach. I can be the token gay man at dinner parties or at social and political events. I can also enjoy being just a senior citizen. Identity is still crucial, no matter what, no matter with whom, and no matter where I am. Once again, it is clear that somehow God always stays in the midst of these messy struggles, often opening a way forward that was not visible or evident before. I have come to trust that fact and be grateful for it.

V

Conscience and Confidence

You say I am repeating
Something I have said before. I shall say it again.
Shall I say it again? In order to arrive there,
To arrive where you are, to get from where you are not,
You must go by a way wherein there is no ecstasy.
In order to arrive at what you do not know
You must go by a way which is the way of ignorance.
In order to possess what you do not possess
You must go by the way of dispossession.
In order to arrive at what you are not
You must go through the way in which you are not.
And what you do not know is the only thing you know
And what you own is what you do not own
And where you are is where you are not.
—T.S. Eliot, Stave III, "East Coker," *Four Quartets*

"May I die in your church?"

The question has haunted me every day since February 1985. Jerome B. "Jerry" Doster of Macon, Georgia, came to my office, covered with purple and brown lesions from Kaposi's sarcoma (a cancer of the lymphatic system), an active case of tuberculosis (TB), and serious wasting syndrome. Breaking his own silence, Jerome came asking only one thing of me: "May I die in your church?" Everything in my life before that moment paled. The desperate sincerity of the question combined with his grim motivation resonated deeply within me. Only in his mid–30s, he had been deathly ill for more than a year. Because of his suffering and hopelessness, he was, as I learned later, planning his suicide for that very day. Jerome merely wanted a priest for Last Rites and a brief funeral.

That's all. Being a man of some style, he had even ordered his printed death cards earlier that morning from world-famous Dallas emporium, Neiman-Marcus.

I had been rector of the Episcopal Church of St. Thomas the Apostle in Dallas for all of six months, holding the notion that the parish needed to be more relevant to the surrounding communities. It was wedged tightly between Dallas Love Field and its historic black community; the opulent Highland Park, located immediately across the street; and, just down from the church on Inwood Road and Mockingbird Lane, a developing *barrio* of Latin American immigrants to which Highland Park was providing some means of employment. I was called by the vestry (the governing board of a parish church) and the bishop to rebuild the congregation, which had fallen on very hard times, and raise up a new community in its midst. But God had another thought. Jerome arrived that day because he had found himself overwhelmed by despair due to the paucity of treatment and therapies for this new disease. There was a good deal of public and particularly religious judgment about those living with what was then known to many as GRID—gay-related immune deficiency—and later came to be known as AIDS, acquired immuno-deficiency syndrome. While it seemed like something quite specific to gay men and their sexual partners, it was more inclusive when you looked into it. From what I had read, women who were partners of injecting drug users and injecting drug users themselves—many of whom were either Black or Latino—were also known to have the same symptoms as gay men. There was so much more we would come to know; however, then there was so very little, and most of it was tempered with racism, homophobia and irrational fear of drug users.

In every sense Jerome had the manner of well-born "Southern Belle." Hailing from Georgia, he preferred a refined and genteel style of life. Looking rather emaciated and decrepit when I met him, I soon learned from photographs that he had cut quite a figure in his earlier days. He was wearing a beard, scraggly though it was, and had sunken eyes in his pockmarked and lesion-afflicted flesh. He had come, in part, because there was buzz in the community that I was welcoming lesbian and gay people to the Church of St. Thomas. The parish offered what some called "radical" hospitality through our open and inclusive welcome of all people and open access to our parish buildings for meetings and support groups for people from the community. Jerome checked it out with the one cleric he knew, retired Bishop Theodore H. McCrea, who coincidentally had ordained me three years before in 1982. Bishop McCrea, also well-known to the gay community of Dallas, advised him to contact me immediately. So Jerome showed up at my doorstep to request what he thought he wanted: the obsequies at the end of life. What happened was more important. After our two-hour visit, where I questioned him about what he needed and how we could support him as a parish, and then after his visiting the parish on several Sundays in the weeks that followed, he came to believe in life. He postponed and later altogether canceled his suicide, deciding instead to let his disease take its natural course, allowing him the fullness of life before his death. He lived another nine months. In that time he inadvertently found himself at the center of a storm which became the moment of decision in a devastating but life-giving parish transition.

Fear of Abandonment

Although I have been an Episcopal priest and in ministry for most of my professional life, I had always held a deep irrational fear of abandonment. That fear is best articulated this way: "Suppose we held church today and nobody came?"

Then it happened. On the second Sunday of September 1985 at St. Thomas, three people showed up to morning liturgy, along with the two employees: the organist and me. Since the previous July many members had come to me weekly, requesting that Jerome be asked to stay at home due to his unknown and potentially dangerous illness. Each request was met with a ringing reminder that at my installation as rector, more than half a year before, I was implored by the preacher and my former mentor in priesthood, Father Charles E. Walling, "You are here to keep the doors open to the whole community. In the name of God, never forget it." While I never considered capitulating to my parishoners' demands and pleas, challenges, and intimidations, I came to learn that no amount of reasoning could deal with the irrational fear of infection. I would take this crucial lesson into account from that time forward. Fear cannot be allayed by facts alone, only accepted for what it is; and, then, maybe, by the grace of God, transformed.

But on this particular Sunday morning, the object of the fear—Jerome—was actually too ill to attend worship. What had been one of the fastest growing churches in the Diocese of Dallas was now becoming the reverse. Over the preceding summer months, more than 170 persons had asked to be transferred to other parishes in Dallas where "AIDS is not present." Graciously as I could, but sadly, they were transferred. However, they could not effectively flee the AIDS epidemic. The effects of AIDS would eventually meet them again and again face-to-face when HIV-positive persons came forward in their new communities over the next decade. All but two members of the vestry resigned, leaving me responsible for virtually everything in the parish. On this Sunday then, with only a handful of worshippers in the church, I officiated at the standard Sunday service, regardless of the number of parishioners present, because it is what I do and have always done, although my worst nightmare had become a reality.

The boycott and flight from the parish had seriously compromised finances—mine and the parish's—which were exceedingly low to non-existent. I had not received a complete paycheck in months due to lack of funds. We—my then-spouse, Kaye, and our two kids, David and Deborah—managed to have something to eat daily, but that was about all. On that morning, a few of the faithful drove up to the church but did not enter, fearful perhaps of siding with a losing cause. With only five of us—a crucifer, server, reader, the organist, and me—I proceeded with the liturgy, complete with the readings, preaching, and teaching, and concluded by celebrating the Holy Eucharist. Keeping with the old traditions we rang the church bells, sending out the word across the larger community around us at the elevation of the bread and wine, intoning the words: "This is the Body of Christ" ... "This is the Blood of Christ."

These Doors Are Open to All People

Then came the miracle as they and I—together—became in that terrible wonderful moment, the body of Christ. One by one a dozen or so churchgoers, who had been waiting in their cars, quietly entered the church during the recitation of the Lord's Prayer to receive these signs of new life. At the end of the service, I was energized and determined, with a congregation now tripled in size. I stated unequivocally, "No matter what happens, these doors will remain open to all people. No matter what!" That pronouncement would be the re-launch; it was our moment of a new beginning.

My enthusiasm would be diminished when the bishop of Dallas, the Right Rev. Donis Dean Patterson, asked me to resign early the next morning. He had received phone calls that Sunday night from disgruntled former vestry members and former parishioners, informing him about the collapsed attendance and financial deprivation created by the departures of so many from St. Thomas. So he appeared at the church early the next day for Morning Prayer, usually led by me daily. When I saw him arrive to a service in which I was usually alone, I admit that I was fearful of what was coming. So I delayed by offering more prayers than the service called for and reciting every psalm and versicle (a short responsive phrase by leader and people responsively) possible: a full half hour of fitful praying.

Then he coughed to get my attention. Neither of us moved. We sat there conversing about the future. He asked for my resignation as the whole place appeared to have collapsed. But riding high from the miracle of the day before, I pointed out to him, as someone who is rather enamored by and knowledgeable of canon law, that without a vestry I could not resign until I had a full complement of a re-constituted vestry. When he asked when this might be, I suggested in about 100 days. It was not the answer he was looking for, but it was my answer, and he reluctantly accepted my terms. (I did not realize at the time that there was a standing offer to the diocese by a real estate developer to purchase the St. Thomas property for a future shopping center. It never happened.) Then I asked for money for me and my family to live on for the next 100 days. He graciously extended that support. In January 1986, about 120 days later, I returned what he had given us, paid our diocesan assessment of fair-share giving, and gave him an additional amount for his discretionary fund to assist other clergy. That was a sweet moment.

During the restart of the St. Thomas congregation, I found myself scrupulously examining anyone who indicated that they wanted to join our membership rolls, having been burned by well-intentioned, enthusiastic parishioners in the first start-up. The word went out in a variety of communities that something unique and rather remarkable was happening at St. Thomas. From time to time, notables from the Dallas area visited to see what we were up to and who was present. I always asked would-be members to indicate their "level of acceptance of lesbians, gays, Blacks, Whites, Latinos, alcoholics and drug addicts, along with HIV-positive persons, because"—stating emphatically and for effect— "all of these people are here and are part of this community of faith. If you have an issue with any, you might want to go somewhere else more agreeable to your nature. Oh yes, and if you are a member, it is crucial that you contribute time, talent, and your treasure to the work of ministry here. Without your support we cannot move forward. Membership has its responsibilities."

A Death and the Community's Rebirth

The more I insisted on my approach to church, the more people wanted to join. Within the last three months of 1985, the parish returned to its previous vigorous growth rate with around 100 folks in the membership, and with a renewed sense of singular purpose and commitment. More people living with HIV/AIDS filled the pews on Sundays in what I described as a "tested" and "open" church and community. The monthly AIDS deaths at St. Thomas would continue to rise unabated for years, mirroring the death rates in Dallas as 150 perished within the confines of St. Thomas alone. I officiated at every funeral and personally attended and counseled every dying person, offering Last Rites and Rites of Healing at every milestone of decline into death.

Jerome died in late November, giving witness to his newfound faith. He struggled for breath, suffering from lung-strangling pneumocystis pneumonia, but asked me, "How do I know when I have received my last Communion?"

I waited a bit, considering this question and its layered meanings, carefully replying, "Every Communion is our last Communion."

He quickly said, "Good, I don't want to miss it."

On the day of his death, I raced over to the hospital after the second service at church. It was a Sunday. He was in his last moments, but being who he was, he waited for my arrival. Even though he was mostly unresponsive, I went ahead with Last Rites, anointing him and praying for a holy death. Then I withdrew a consecrated host from the previous mass, which I had brought in my hospital kit. I touched it to his lips, before I consumed it, saying, "Now, Jerome, you have received your last Communion among us. Before this day is over you will be dining with Christ in paradise." His fragile lips moved toward a smile, and then he gave up his breath and died. Thus the life of the man who had changed my life and that of an entire community forever ended in quiet and peace.

The pace of responding to the ever-increasing demands of those living with HIV/AIDS, along with the usual demands of being the only parish priest in a fast-growing urban parish, was often causing me to keep 80- to 100-hour weeks. Not good for a family, I admit. Looking back on that time, I wonder how we got through it. I confess, most of the time it was a mystery. Whenever I came to a contradiction or stopping place, roadblock or ditch, I found myself saying: "It's your call, God. You called me into this, no one else did, so let's figure it out. What do we need to do next?" Within a day or two there was a solution of some kind on the horizon. When asked by a reporter what it was like to serve in such relentless ministry, I compared working in AIDS to riding a surfboard ... in a tidal wave. "I can hear the roar," I said. "The ride is death-defying. One false move and you are gone ... history."

Without necessarily seeking it, I had become a community AIDS educator. Our parish had become a home for training laypersons and clergy alike in the care and support of people living with AIDS. Over the years, as our credibility grew, we became the center of the Dallas-area AIDS Interfaith Network, as well as the weekly meeting place of the area case management system, known as AIDS Arms Network, of which I was a co-founder. The parish was a beacon of light in a very fearful and tentative dark environment.

A Hopeful Future

Even today, the parish of St. Thomas continues with this ministry with its second rector since my departure in 1989, leading the way in which a faith community can honor and give witness to the Gospel in the twenty-first century. It is a vibrant community, located on beautifully landscaped grounds, with attractive efficient buildings. The parish has committed itself to a hopeful future, using its buildings and grounds to give witness to the green revolution and even having its own parish produce garden. Jerome's remains, along with the dozens and dozens of others also interred in the columbarium, still give witness to the monumental change wrought by HIV/AIDS more than three decades later. The witness of faithfulness and commitment has not been silenced but has become ever more eloquent.

As for me, since that day to this, now 35 years later, I have never known a day without someone living with HIV/AIDS in my life. I continue to offer counsel and guidance to the young on how to prevent the spread of HIV, and comfort and solace to the infected and affected. Because of what happened at St. Thomas, I also have become fearless when people withdraw support from a parish or any other enterprise and have proceeded with impunity.

Escorting the president of the House of Deputies of the Episcopal Church, Dr. Pamela Chinnis, on the AIDS Memorial Quilt on the Mall in Washington, D.C., October 1996.

The ministry that began at St. Thomas and parishes like it gave rise to the creation of a variety of institutions, among them the National Episcopal AIDS Coalition, which is still functioning. The work also called me out again and again into more challenging settings, from the national epidemic in the United States to the epicenter of the global pandemic in South Africa, as well as from the U.S. government response to the global AIDS program at the World Health Organization (WHO) and from a local parish response in Dallas to an international response by the Anglican Communion. But the story of Jerome and his challenges and witness has been spoken of on every continent around the world by me and others who are touched by the story and because of testimony in magazines, newspapers and other social media and has provided ongoing inspiration to millions engaged in care for people living with HIV/AIDS over the years.

Walking down a street in Nairobi, Kenya, in 2003, I was stopped by a man who yelled out, "Father, I saw you on television. You're the priest who opened his parish to people like me." I listened to his story of being a Seventh Day Adventist who was living with AIDS. I had been interviewed ten years before by the Seventh Day Adventist international television system about what had happened in Dallas in the 1980s. The interview had apparently been re-broadcast repeatedly around the world.

What I have learned? Faithfulness in apparent small things over the long haul is faithfulness in great things over a lifetime. No one could have imagined what was in store for us when Jerome asked, "May I die in your church?"

My answer today, "Of course, but you can also live in our love."

VI

Calling and Commitment

All real living is meeting. The relation to the Thou is direct.
No system of ideas, no foreknowledge, and no fancy intervener
  between I and Thou.
The memory itself is transformed as it plunges out of its isolation
  into the unity of the whole.
No aim, no lust, and no anticipation intervene between I and
  Thou.
—Martin Buber, *I and Thou*

The young South African Zulu doctor turned to me suddenly and said, "You're a priest." This happened during a visit to the rude and decrepit buildings of the old Lutheran Missionary Hospital in a small South African village. He continued, "I need you now to go back through every room and ward and pray with every single patient. They need your prayers tonight." This was more an order than a request. It was 2001, and I was relatively new in South Africa, having been there for only about eight weeks. I protested, saying, "I don't speak any of these languages, and they may well not understand English." Looking disgusted, he said, "Do you know God?" I nodded silently. "Then give them God. It is all they have. And besides, you're a priest, and everyone here knows what that is."

I was in Hlabisa, a small municipality of about 600 folk, of which an estimated 350 were HIV positive. Sitting in north central Kwazulu-Natal, the little village is the smallest in the Umkhanyakude District, near Durban. The *New York Times* in 2001 described this place as the epicenter of the HIV/AIDS global pandemic. It was. I was there with friends from the States, who were part of a team filming for Ted Koppel's

Nightline. While they were there to film, I was there primarily to learn, accompanying them in my new role as a priest and head of the HIV/AIDS program from the Office of the Archbishop of Cape Town. There are many Anglicans in Zululand, including the king of the Zulus, so being there as a priest would add some sanctity and dignity to the process and facilitate our getting closer to people more rapidly. It did, but not in ways I expected.

This young doctor, a noble-looking Zulu professional whose name I have long since forgotten, was clearly very successful. He lived in Johannesburg but found himself "coming home" to Zululand once a month to treat the hundreds of men, women, and children in this depressed and resource-poor district. His spare, primitive office was nothing more than a concrete shell of a garage, which had a wooden screen for a front door and a single bulb hanging precariously by a thin wire blowing about in the dusky Zulu winter evening. His drug dispensary was a doorless closet, and his waiting room a splintered bench by the front door. But his commitment to treat his people as best he could was clearly the most important thing to him. He told me, "I don't believe in God. How can I, given the horror we have here? Every other person is HIV positive. I came back because my people need me … and I am the only one who will come. Besides, my sister is also HIV positive. So it is the least that I can do."

The Epicenter of the Pandemic

Hlabisa, located in the middle of an old game preserve, had a hospital built in the nineteenth century that was now a wreck of a place under government management. The Lutheran medical missionaries, active in this area for nearly one hundred years, left when the former, all-white, apartheid government passed the Bantu Education Act in 1953, which legalized large portions of apartheid. The local missionaries would not respect the laws, so they closed their mission hospitals and handed them over to the South African federal government. But government didn't provide healthcare. "When AIDS broke out," the doctor explained, "the village cleaned up the aging facility and staffed it with volunteers and members of the Mothers' Union." On this day, the hospital built for 40 persons had more than 120 men, women, and children gathered there. The children were primarily those who were born in the hospital and had remained because of their disease. They were known as "boarder babies." Throughout the facility, aging beds and the exceedingly thin mattresses supported two people in the same bed. Below, on pallets, were another two or three patients who were slightly better off. From the tell-tale heavy coughing and spewing, it was evident that a great deal of TB was running rampant through the place—often a natural byproduct of AIDS. To my surprise and then horror, there was no negative airflow system to manage or minimize the spread of TB infection throughout the hospital.

The air was, in fact, redolent with TB and other bacteria and overlain with the sickly-sweet scent of vomit and diarrhea. The acrid ammonia scent of urine, often found sitting in glass bottles by each bed, added to the intense aromatic atmosphere. The distinctive scent of human sweat was tempered with cooking odors. Among them, small kerosene or paraffin cook stoves were alight and, of course, there was the ubiquitous *pap* (*mieliepap*—coarsely ground maize of porridge consistency) that can be eaten anytime by adding vegetables and chili or sugar and butter. Pap can be served in a firm, dry, or crumbly state, as in *putu pap*, or smooth, as the easy-to-swallow *slap pap*. This South African staple for the poor was served to all bedridden patients who could hold down their food. The more ambulatory were seated at long tables near the ward, nursing their pap with glasses of Lucozade (a carbonated energy drink invented in Britain almost a century before, containing high amounts of glucose, citric acid, and lactic acid). It is said that this combination is "good for you" and will give the needed essential nutrition and energy, especially to one who is particularly ill. The whole vile combination of scents overpowered me, bringing me to a nauseated state by the end of the evening. I also somehow realized that I would one day be grateful for the intensity of life hitting me quite so hard. Each moment spent there would be about real life, life clinging desperately to life, and curiously, about a holy life, pretty or not. It was about real, honest-to-God life.

It was the height of winter. The harsh winds blew off the Indian Ocean, chilling the compound, moaning unceremoniously through the walls and ceiling joists. The dry brown-and-gold bush and weed blew wildly, creating a hissing sound across the dark and treeless hillsides. An occasional lion could be seen roaming for food as a small harem of zebra charged off in the opposite direction. Into this place I was invited—no, ordered—to go by this brash young doctor who seemed preoccupied by other things. I was assigned and summarily dismissed…. To pray.

The Night of Prayer

And so it began, some three hours of praying and imploring God to do something, moving quietly from person to person as they consumed their evening supply of pap being lovingly prepared by a family member over cooking fires in the hallway, the interior yard of the hospital, or in the very sparse, tired kitchen. And there I was sitting, standing, or kneeling beside each person, speaking in quiet, reassuring tones, inviting them to pray. Few spoke English, and I spoke virtually no Zulu. But by evening's end I learned some of the meaningful names of God: *Unkulunkulu* (God of the Zulu Bible), *Usomadla* (all-powerful one), and *Usimakade* (the one who has always been there).

Somehow moving between these forms of address to the deity seemed to make sense to me, and prompted even the sickest of these to correct my poor attempts at Zulu pronunciation. But that meant engagement and connection. There was a palpable gentleness and recognition from each person as I sought nothing from them and wished only for their well-being through this tangible act of praying with each one. From time to time an African hymn would arise among the ill and their visitors in the ward and would continue quietly as I prayed, coming to a crescendo when the time for prayer was completed. Even as sick as the people were, hands were quietly clapped as if to drive the darkness away. The hours flowed by in a blur of tears and smiles, hand-holding, hymn-singing, and praying—prayers of solace, prayers of pleading, prayers of demand, or of capitulation to the will of God.

Finally, thoroughly exhausted and feeling empty inside as I completed my rounds—at nearly 10 p.m.—the doctor reappeared from the darkness, accompanied by gusts of howling wind. A brief, almost understated smile appeared on his face. He seemed pleased that I had completed my assignment for the evening. The hospital grew quiet as the lights were lowered and the kerosene lanterns extinguished. As we walked up the hospital drive, there was a sudden lull in the wind. I asked him, "Why? Why me? Why tonight? Why in this way?"

That's All You Can Do

He looked deeply into my eyes and said, "Because you're a priest and that is all that you can do for them. And you accept that at face value. I am a physician, an educated and informed man. And indeed, while I grew up in the Church, I am no longer a churchman. Science got the best of me. Besides, out here we are constantly up against death!"

It still didn't answer my question. In that momentous silence, looking up to a silvery moon as wisps of cloud skittered by, he admitted, almost in a spirit of confession, "We ran out of all the meds at midday today.... And we had hoped that something would come from the government stores in Durban. But nothing, nothing came. We are without any supplies or treatment and may or may not even get them tomorrow. With no treatment, all we have is their will and God's. Your prayers tonight are all that they have here to make it through the night." Then the wind roared again, now with a great moan in hedgerows and shrubs as if to accentuate the horror. The dried rustling grasses hissed as the fearful serpent of death slithered away. Tears came quickly at the sheer enormity of the task and the magnitude of the crisis.

All they have is prayer? I kept muttering to myself. *All they have is prayer? All they have is prayer.* It was that night that I came to a fuller understanding of my calling and my acceptance of that calling as a priest of the Church. It is a call, ultimately, to helplessness and vulnerability as much as it is to prayer and raising signposts of hope. In that moment I came to understand, maybe for the first time in my professional life, that my prayers, as paltry and as meaningless as they had often seemed to me, were actually worth something to someone else. While I was skillful in the art of public prayer and had been struggling to develop a deeper meaningful life of personal prayer, rarely did these worlds intersect as they did that night. Liturgical prayer in public worship often summarized the best of religious intention, but only occasionally met the demands of the moment and the profound need of a people. On this

In Soweto, the Rev. Charles May blesses Canon Ted Karpf before preaching on HIV/AIDS in the heart of South Africa, 2002.

night, using the forms of prayer for the sick that I knew by rote, I found myself transported in time to a place in eternity, where the deepest longings and needs of those for whom I prayed were received. By the power to hear and understand the people in utter need, all I could do and perhaps that God did was to respond.

Digging In

My favorite Presbyterian humanist religious thinker, Frederick Buechner, in his 1973 book, *Wishful Thinking*, describes vocation (calling) as "from the Latin *vocare*, to summon or call, [meaning] the work a man [sic] is called to do by God…. By and large a good rule for finding out is this: The kind of work God usually calls you to is the kind of work (a) that you need most to do and (b) that the world most needs to have done…. The place God calls you is the place where your deep gladness and the world's deep hunger meet."

Buechner's statement works for me, as there has always been the daily reality of experiencing my deepest gladness in the work. I knew that I was on the right track of living into this reality of my calling by being called to South Africa and doing this agonizing work. I would have preferred a place above the fray of suffering, like organizing other people and planning how they would meet the challenges of the pandemic, but here I was being told to continue to identify with and live into my own helplessness. I could do nothing to extend anyone's life that night other than to show up and be present to the suffering and need. This is what I had done in Dallas nearly 20 years before through the early years of AIDS and its terrible extended season of death. With so many deaths in four years in my parish community, I believed then that I was at the epicenter in Dallas. In hindsight now, it was just boot camp for the global pandemic. Now I was at the epicenter in sub–Saharan Africa, and still, all I could do was what I had always done: just show up and be present.

Being present does not always come quite so naturally. I often want to make something happen to alleviate the pain or mitigate the suffering. I often want to achieve something as the payoff for showing up. Calling—*vocatio* (a call or summons), often thought of as an otherworldly mystical experience, and it can be for some—is more like an itch that refuses to be satisfied. Just below the surface it sat there, reminding me that something was waiting to be done. Until the demand was met, life would not be wholly satisfying.

I'd always had a sense that what I was doing was somehow important enough to be consistent with what I understood God to be summoning me to do. That night in Zululand I found a larger purpose for this understanding of calling. Fortunately it was often the work needed in the community, in the Church, or in the world—through government service, through volunteer work, at work through an occupation, or through my witness in the Church. Somehow all of this was understood as vocation. The very derivation of calling as *vocare* or *vocatio* has a sense of being summoned or called out by a higher power, or at least an authority larger than oneself. So it was not a big leap to understand that this word was applied to the sense of a godly calling, as the Church would refer to it. However one understands calling, though, it is entirely driven by the social, cultural, and spiritual context into which one is called.

Calling into action, even the action of waiting in silence, allowed me to enter the mystery of what God is up to in this world. This experience contrasted to my previous life where I was primarily an observer and recorder of events. Sitting on the sidelines, I told the story but did not live it.

Observing/Engaging

At age 16, in 1964, I focused on being a journalist. Somewhere in mid-adolescence I discovered that I had a way with words. I wrote for local and area metropolitan newspapers in Fort Worth, Texas. Waiting until I grew up was not for me. At 16 I began working for a small community daily, covering high school sports. I also learned to tell stories about the community and particularly about the youth. By the time I entered college, I had already been writing professionally (that is, for money; a dime per column inch of newspaper copy) for three years. I had been on the high school paper and received a college scholarship from the Texas Gridiron Club to major in journalism. Soon after entering college I worked on the college paper, a weekly, and in developing, writing, and editing a monthly publication for Goodwill Industries of Fort Worth. The summer of 1967 I was working for the area's largest newspaper, the *Fort Worth Star-Telegram*. That fall, I moved to the *Fort Worth Press* as editor of the teen pages. That assignment lasted nine months—the school year.

In May 1968, national events—two political assassinations (Dr. Martin Luther King, Jr., and Senator Robert Kennedy) within eight weeks and increasing national protest over the war in Vietnam—overtook the news. I had just taken a job with *The Decatur Daily* in Decatur, Alabama. Located on the banks of the Tennessee River in northern Alabama, Decatur had a population of about 36,000, of which 20 percent was black. While primarily a county paper for Morgan County, Alabama, the paper reported stories for much of the northern half of Alabama: from the Tennessee, Mississippi, and Georgia borders. I also submitted freelance stories for the Associated Press, particularly about former Alabama Governor George C. Wallace; Lurleen B. Wallace, the spouse of

George Wallace who served briefly as governor until her death in May 1968; and Albert P. Brewer of Decatur, former lieutenant governor, who had recently succeeded her. Mr. Wallace was by then running for president as the nominee of the American Independent Party. He was stirring up a great deal of racist rhetoric, yet if one listened carefully, he was proposing a reasonably practical populist agenda, which some of the African Americans in Alabama could support. It all became a contradiction for me.

The Ku Klux Klan was also very active during these years. Frightened and fascinated, I witnessed cross-burnings and saw grown men covering their identities in white bedsheets, strutting around large burning crosses and spewing their racial epithets of hatred. I smelled the objectionable scent of suspicion and revulsion. With all the national turmoil of that spring of 1968, and the accompanying trauma of riots, demonstrations, and outrage in the face of two assassinations—King and Kennedy—here I was in the heart of the redneck-racist belt of Alabama. Yet in nearby Huntsville was NASA's Marshall Space Flight Center, staffed with some of the top refugee and exiled scientists, who were working on behalf of the U.S. space program. The contrasts were overwhelming, and yet I was an observer. Also, by way of contrast, in the real hard-scrabble, dusty communities and towns of North Alabama, black and white folk lived side by side in relative peace and with uneasy acceptance and grudging respect about the status quo of American life. All—Black and White—felt left out and neglected for some reason or other.

These contrasts and contradictions became my daily working realities. It was a heady time to be a young reporter. At once I was covering national politics, at the county courthouse with its crusty, cigar-smoking, "good old boy" judges, and unqualified legal hacks representing the population. I spent my days digging up local stories about racism, war resistance, local tragedies, car crashes, shootings, and the general mayhem around us. It was all a bit surreal in this place which could have been the backdrop of a gothic novel about the Old South. Where was William Faulkner or Tennessee Williams?

I found myself in an emotional and spiritual tug-of-war between rapid professional success as a newspaper reporter and this as-of-yet ill-defined faith and sense of personal calling to ministry. The conflict became even clearer when I was invited to take a reporting position on the highly reputable *Huntsville Times*. A quick study, I had learned a good deal about the relatively poor but respectful common life of North Alabama. I had also delved into the background issues facing these communities, trying to get behind the racism and culture, national debates of war and peace, and searing national election primaries. Thus, after only eight weeks at the *Daily*, I was offered the job at the *Times* before the end of August 1968. I turned it down because I was already growing depressed and impatient with newspapering as a profession and with the industry itself. I carefully considered my dissatisfaction based on the growing unease of merely observing and recording facts to tell a story. My desire was to be about living into the changes I wanted—reshaping society which was in chaos—not just documenting it. I wanted to engage in politics, not just write about change. I wanted to feel fulfilled in doing the work of making the country more open for all people.

I was having this ongoing conversation about my discontent with several friends in Decatur. Opal and Namon Florence were faithful members of the Church of Christ; Louie Namie, a Lebanese Maronite Christian immigrant and owner of the local grocery; and iconoclast Dick Harris, a scion of the rich and powerful in Decatur who ran the local cotton gin. I often dined with the Florences on simple Southern country food: grits, fried green tomatoes, corn on the cob, and a fresh-picked salad of whatever was ripe in their garden. It was comforting and reassuring to just have a good meal. Their son and daughter were both married and had established families in nearby Huntsville. Namon was a teacher and Opal a secretary, soon to be retired. Both were employed at the Decatur Trade School (now Calhoun Community College). I had met them, along with Dick and Nancy Harris, two years before in the summer of 1966, when I was working as a Bible salesman for the Southwestern Company. I didn't sell many Bibles but I did come through that summer with some new good friends. I managed to keep up contact with them over the next two years (1966–68). When the position came open at *The Decatur Daily*, they encouraged me to accept it, and that gave me friends on arrival.

Opal and Namon had apparently watched me struggle with this itch about religion and ministry and offered their insights and support. In turn they introduced me to Louie Namie, whom they knew to be a man of deep loyal faith. He was a local grocer whose store I patronized. Over time he and I engaged in deep philosophical conversations about faith and the importance of ritual. Eventually he invited me for a Sunday trip to the Maronite Christian basilica in Birmingham. We spent a day sojourning to and from Birmingham and while there witnessed a beautiful liturgy that filled my senses and soul in ways that nothing had before.

Meanwhile Dick Harris and I would get together at the end of each week when I would debrief him about what was happening in Decatur. He knew everyone and knew best how to handle them, particularly the politicians. He helped me understand what was happening and often the "why" below the apparent story being told. Dick was an iconoclast and a skeptic. In our tobacco-smoke-filled and bourbon-soaked conversations, I felt his insistent urging to keep engaging the questions of religion and faith. From Dick I learned that merely acting the iconoclast did not necessarily indicate a lack of faith. Many find themselves in a similar position. In truth, he just disliked and distrusted most institutions. I now feel the same way.

Not one of these friends said "go to church" per se, but they heard me out as I struggled with the Christian expression of community and clear tenets of inclusion and God's love for all. Somewhere along this journey, I had come to believe that I needed to be an "official" ordained clergy person of some kind, though I never had thoughts of it before. On one hand I saw myself as a somewhat traditional preacher/minister— though I couldn't imagine that my deeply held struggles over my beliefs and the ghost of my sexuality would be welcomed, understood, or even tolerated. On the other hand, perhaps I thought I might better serve as a nonconformist street evangelist. It was clear then and it is still true that I am more at home on the streets or in the marketplace than I am in church. I had attended a Methodist church from the time when, as a child, I could take myself there on foot. So in this stressful moment, it was no surprise to me that I attended the local Methodist church on some Sundays. After a service I met with the preacher, who, after talking with me about my conflict with God and calling, suggested that I preach on some Sunday "to see what it was like." An odd response to a virtual stranger, but I guess he could tell that this conflict was very deep and very real and that my life and calling hung in the balance.

I recall that I preached a sermon on peace-making in that chaotic summer of 1968. It was more like a cross between a naive but heartfelt hippie love poem and an attempt to preach the gospel laden with fierce judgment and social critique of the war mongers (that would have been anyone agreeing with the government) and not much peace offered for anyone else. It was received for the effort it was. The response from the congregation was mostly silence. I had to acknowledge that I was obviously preaching more for me and my journey. Harris suggested that I had attempted "to talk the gospel to death." Louie could just say, "We don't do it like this in the Lebanese church." The Florences were gracious but tight-lipped. My first sermon was both a dud and spark.

An inquiry from my local draft board in Fort Worth arrived several days after my attempt to be a preacher in church. In August 1968, I received a letter asking what I was doing in Alabama and why I was not attending college or university. After all, attending school was the reason for which I was deferred from the draft and military service. On top of the spiritual quandary I was already in, it was evident that I now had to deal with the reality of the draft and the war in Vietnam and my place in it or not. Within days, I gave notice and packed my bags to return to Fort Worth in time to gain late admission back into Texas Wesleyan College that September.

Traveling in my well-worn, two-tone green 1954 Chevy Deluxe Coupe, I arrived in Fort Worth after three-and-a-half days of driving. I went up to our house—which I had just left in April—and tried to open the door. It was locked. I knocked. A stranger answered. It seems that Mom and Dad had forgotten to inform me that they had moved during the summer. So I found myself going home humbled and conflicted and now to a new residence by another way. First, though, was to find a telephone booth to call them and find out where they were now located. It was awkward and upsetting as they explained their assumption that I would be gone for a long time. They had forgotten to mention that they had grown used to the fact that only one of the three sons lived at home, so they decided on a whim to change their home location to match. This was to have been their "new nearly empty nest," but one of their birds had apparently just flown back. It was me. I was given the unused living room to "camp out" in until I found a better situation elsewhere.

Going to Church

Returning to Texas Wesleyan, I was meeting the requirement for an educational deferment, but I went further to pursue this "religion thing," as I called it. I met with the chair of the Religion Department, Dr. Alice Wonders, a giant in the Methodist Church of Texas and particularly in Fort Worth. A lay female PhD Biblical scholar who had shaped more clergy than anyone dares to tell, she raised up several generations of clergy who were guided under her tutelage. I was yet another. I explained this unnerving sense of call that I really didn't know what to do with. Of course, she suggested several religion and Bible courses I would need in order to attend theological graduate school or seminary. And, yes, she noted that it would be good to align with a local church so I could see what working in one would be like. She then recommended me for a job there in Fort Worth. Within a week I was standing in a congregation, attempting to put on the countenance of youth minister. It was awkward and strange and done rather poorly.

I had not been to church weekly since early in high school. I had two years of experience in a world that was anything but religious. Nonetheless, the minister took a chance on me. The kids were great and several became friends—I was, after all, only 18 months or so older than most of the high school seniors and something like 28 months older than most of the juniors. The partner of one of those kids is still a close friend to this day. Yes, I keep people in my life for a very long time.

That was also the autumn of 1968 when Richard M. Nixon was elected president. The country had divided itself by generations. We young "Baby Boomers" were hardly interested in or supportive of the Vietnam War, while our parents seemingly declared war on us by the volume and force of their disagreement. And being 20, I was not yet old enough to vote in those days, though my peers were being sent into battle to die. By the time 1969 rolled around, more than 20 people I had known since childhood were dead. This was a lot of loss for one who knew so relatively little about life and death. It marked me. By the time I retired 45-plus years later, I had lost literally hundreds of friends and colleagues: first to the Vietnam War; then to HIV/AIDS and other catastrophic illnesses; and now, finally, to aging. But the whole debacle of Vietnam marked my Waterloo moment with loss and death, subsequently galvanizing my soul ever after around matters of distrust for government and leadership.

I was old enough to realize that the way my parents raised me was not necessarily healthy or even appropriate. My father's loyalty to his Republican and racist interests and stridently anti–Communist rhetoric made me angry, particularly as his attitude was so righteous. I considered the institutions of government corrupt and deceptive. Protests and movements were fractious and often short-lived. On the personal side, I yearned for, yet feared, being loved by anyone. I was hopelessly attracted and frustrated by the conflicting feelings I had with several men and could not even speak of it. And I was terrified of how I felt about myself. I was no different than millions of other "Boomers" in their twenties. But I was also caught up in the struggle about faith, fervor, and calling.

By the spring I had been fired from my church job. I simply did not know how to build a youth program in church, or outside of it for that matter. I thought I still wanted to be in church, even when the preaching was boring and the service numbing. It was then that I found my first real mentor in the Church. His name was C. Bourdon Smith— "Bourdon" to many—a Methodist pastor at Whaley United Methodist Church in the heart of Gainesville, Texas, about 65 miles north of Fort Worth.

The town population was about 16,000. It had the distinction of being the first stop in Texas of the Texas Chief, a passenger train of the Atchison, Topeka, and Santa Fe (ATSF) Railway out of Chicago, and the last Texas town where the train stopped on its way to Chicago. Gainesville really got its identity from the railroad as the Katy Railroad from Kansas arrived in the 1880s, coincidentally at the end of the Indian Wars. It was only then that the town began to prosper. In 1920, Gainesville got another boost with the discovery of oil in nearby Callisburg. Thus the Depression wasn't as bad on Gainesville as it might have been, for the town became a center of oil and gas drilling in North Central Texas.

Whaley Church was a big barn of a place, two blocks from the railroad station and at the "new end"—the East End—of town. The well-established First Methodist Church was in the center of town on a silk-stocking street. Clearly the bankers and lawyers were there, and the rest of us were on the east side. The Reverend Smith was intrigued with me and my sense of calling. He proceeded to instruct me in the basics of faith and of churchmanship. As part of his teaching, he included me in every Sunday worship, allowing me to lead the service after a few months. By Labor Day, I was leading and preaching the Sunday service during his vacation in 1969. I lived in a little church-owned shanty behind the church, adjacent to the parsonage. So we were a tidy little community.

Bourdon, a West Texan who spoke with the distinctive West Texas twang, explained a down-to-earth theology to me that I later learned was wonderfully advanced in the direction of process theology. This theology made its appearance in the mid–twentieth century, departing from classical Christian thinking around the nature of God, who is either primordial and totally removed from the world and unchanging, or who is completely engaged with the world and thus is constantly changing. Some conservative Christians believe this thinking is actually non–Christian. It isn't. It arises out of the philosophy of Alfred North Whitehead and was advocated and expanded by Schubert Ogden and John Cobb. Whitehead, a world-famous mathematician and philosopher, emigrated to the U.S. from the U.K. in 1924 and taught to the end of his life at Harvard.

Through the hard lens of process theology and straight from his heart, telling stories and offering illustrations right out of our lives, Bourdon delivered his understanding of Christian scripture. He was often condemned by the uppity folk who thought that his sermons were just too common. He incurred a fair bit of resistance from the leadership of the Annual Conference and their "high-falutin'" ways. Bourdon was a man's man, but also a man of the people: prophetic and insightful in the ways he understood the faith and value of our experience in making the most basic to the most important decisions about our lives. I loved him and everything about him. His family was a mess, but he loved them for the unique people they were. His wife, Jackie, was deeply unhappy being a preacher's wife, especially in Gainesville, Texas. She saw herself as an urban, enlightened earth mother leading us out of the captivity of our country ways and narrow cultural biases. They would divorce some years later.

Gainesville gave me a great deal, especially a sense of self and an identity as a would-be cleric. There were wonderful, loving parishioners, some of whom really guided and assisted me. I received great mentoring for, and modeling of, the pastoral office by Bourdon, and then there was his inspired preaching and interpretation of scripture. He offered an invitation that I took enthusiastically to participate as a peer in a great, open, and accepting laboratory to explore worship, leadership, ministerial identity, prayer, and mysticism. This time also provided my first cross-cultural experience in ministry when I was invited to preach in the local Black Pentecostal Holiness Church, pastored by the Whaley Church custodian, Hulen Gooden (known in the community as the "Walkin' Bible"). He and his family loved me and I them.

When I preached that first time, it was on a particularly hot July Sunday afternoon. I stepped up into the pulpit after about an hour of congregational singing and praying. I completed my sermon in about 15 minutes, wrapping it up with a rollicking good song. Hulen quietly said to me, "Nice beginning, Brother Ted. Now come on and preach to us God's Holy Word today!" I was floored, but as they say in Texas, it was then that I "commenced to preachin'," ad-libbing and summarizing every good sermon I had ever heard and could remember. After 45 minutes of this, often interrupted by spontaneous seizures causing some of the members to fall onto the floor and others to faint into the arms of the nearby faithful or sing holiness songs inspired by the Holy Ghost, I got the rhythm and brought the whole exercise to a thunderous conclusion, calling down the saints and angels on the whole community. Hulen was delighted and danced his way down the aisle in celebration of a sacred moment in the church.

At staff meeting the next morning, Hulen reported to Bourdon and the church secretary, Bernice, that I had "brought down the Spirit." He then announced like a prophet of old, "I think our brother, Ted, has been baptized in the Holy Ghost! It is obvious to anyone with eyes to see and ears to hear that he is absolutely called to be a preacher forever!" Bourdon was impressed, and Bernice touched and quietly amused. This was the summer before my senior year in college and the completion of my applications to theological graduate school. I didn't know what to make of Hulen's clearly heartfelt pronouncement, and Bourdon would bring it up from time to time, teasing me about it. But it is still a powerful memory of what calling can mean and what can issue from a heart bent toward God. It comes up every time I want to throw in the towel and quit, which has been more often than I care to admit over nearly five decades. The demands of living and the precarious place that clergy hold in our society often lead me to reconsider what I have done and the cost of it in terms of comfort and stability.

Through the rest of my college career—the next 18 months—I commuted between Fort Worth and Gainesville, heading up on Friday middays and back to Fort Worth early on Monday mornings to attend classes at Wesleyan. I was beginning to live into the identity of a minister, struggling and occasionally succeeding at making up for two missing years of intellectual and spiritual formation. I took religion and humanities courses by doubling up in the summer and fall and doing a directed study in January 1970 to bring my degree to a full double major of religion and humanities with a minor in journalism and mass communication, graduating with honors.

Meanwhile, when I wasn't working in church or editing the college paper, I spent every free moment protesting the war in Vietnam, including going to Washington twice to protest at the Pentagon. The moral reasoning for this war, I believed, was deeply flawed. The whole experience, though, marked a brutal generational divide between my father and his peers and me and my peers. I could not find any justification for invading a foreign nation during its own civil war and calling it "defending freedom in America." Besides, Richard Nixon was president and we were, as history has shown, rightly paranoid about his abuses of power, military might, and authority. Now that I was 21, this divide would assert itself in my lack of trust for those in power, and yet I still desired to be trusted and recognized by the same people in power.

Training for Ministry

Filled with social and political outrage, I would soon be going to graduate theological school. I was sufficiently non-conformist to not accept the wise counsel of most of my faculty about learning to fit in, though I accepted willingly the counsel of Dr. Wonders, who "got me" and gently turned me in the direction of where to go for graduate professional education. I had been awarded significant scholarships and offers from Duke Divinity School, Perkins School of Theology at SMU in Dallas, Claremont in California, and Union Theological in New York.

I chose none of them, instead deciding to attend Boston University School of Theology. Called the "School of the Prophets" since the 1890s, it was the place where Dr. Martin Luther King, Jr., received his doctorate in ethics and theology. BU was also known to many Methodists as the "Bishops School," as many of the powerful bishops of the denomination graduated there, including my own bishop in Dallas. In every respect it was non-conformist, liberal, and considered by some to be radical. After all, Dr. Walter Muelder, an ethicist, was known across the Methodist Church as the "Pink Dean," having been a war resister in the Second World War and in recent years had been providing sanctuary in the precincts of the divinity school and the university chapel to Vietnam War draft resisters. The legendary mystic and prophet, the Rev. Howard Thurman, had been dean of BU's Marsh Chapel as well, though he had recently retired. Yes, there was a great legacy and heritage at Boston, and it was as far from Fort Worth in culture, tradition, and experience as one could possibly go. Because my mother's roots were in Boston, specifically on the South Shore in Quincy, I thought I needed exposure to my Northeastern family ties. We had already been living in Texas for seven years, and I wanted to be immersed once more into the Northeastern mentality.

This notion of being called to ministry would be tested again and again. Because Boston is in secular New England, the more traditional churchly language of conservatives and fundamentalists—ubiquitous in the South and Southwest—was rarely recognized or spoken of, much less used. Thus I became a bit of an anomaly for BU. Early on I received the title of being the class "dogmatic," meaning traditionalist. Because of my curious Texas and East Coast contortions of accent and colloquialisms, I stood out as being different. By Northern standards, I was considered by some to be a bumpkin for speaking out in apparently unenlightened ways. I confess I was scared to death, but that is why I chose the place. I would have to grow.

Because of where I came from, I was challenged throughout my theological and professional training on the legitimacy of my liberal social and political leanings. Academic rigor and intellectual accountability were demanded by faculty in all of my classes at Boston University and also at Harvard Divinity where I studied. How one thought through a problem and how one thought through theology and how one explained it with rigor and consistency were demanded at every turn. It was often a matter of "to hell with what you believe; we want to know what you think and how you express it coherently, in keeping with the two-millennia tradition of Christian apologetics" (from the Greek *apologia* meaning "in defense of"). This was the academic and historic heritage of the Boston institutions, and particularly BU School of Theology within the United Methodist Church. Fortunately, I was enrolled in what was reputed to be a three-year double-major degree (Sacred Theology Master and Bachelor of Divinity) program. It was a good program in that I would actually have four or five years to complete it, instead of the usual three.

At the end of my first year, 1971, I was ordained a deacon in the United Methodist Church. In order to understand my own chosen disciplines, I had been producing a weekly religious program on public television in Boston since arriving in September 1970. It would later become a Peabody Award–winner under my successor. In those studios, though, I learned about religious broadcasting and mass communications, and the challenges that I would face should I try to make a career in that field. The downside was that it felt too much like writing for the newspapers again.

In the summer of 1971, I was chosen by the Vermont Ecumenical Council and Bible Society to develop a ministry to commune dwellers in Vermont. That three-month journey introduced me to the possibilities of organizing ministry to communities, as well as bringing public health messages, which much later in my career would mark my ability to hold religion and public health in tandem. The Vermont Department of Public Health issued a manual for commune dwellers on basic hygiene and how to build outdoor latrines, as these children of the '60s were trying to eke out livings in the wildernesses of Vermont, not knowing the basic health and hygiene issues. Commune dwellers seemed rather adept at sharing infections (STDs notwithstanding) from poorly drained latrines, poor food preparation, and bug-infested bedding from infrequent bed-changes and too many strangers "crashing" for the night, along with the use of unwashed towels. Transmission of unwanted infections was guaranteed.

The manual was a bit of a heads-up to a generation of young people who'd not necessarily thought about these things before. They were mostly middle-class kids whose parents had given them lives without such concerns. The manual served as a tool, a means to gain access to these communities so that I could further assess needs and offer support from local and area faith communities and some limited assistance, from cash to food, diapers to detergent. It was also during that first year of theology school that I tried, again in vain, to serve as youth minister in a Methodist church, though I was dismissed before spring break in March. But that exercise seemed crucial to finding my Episcopal roots in Boston, first at Trinity Church in Copley Square, led by the Rev. Theodore Parker Ferris, and later at Emmanuel Church, where the Rev. Al Kershaw was leading a cutting-edge ministry in the arts.

After that crazy summer and the manic first 13 months in Boston, I was thoroughly exhausted and had no idea what I was doing or why. I secured a leave of absence from the School of Theology and traveled overseas for the next year, interning for six months of it at the World Council of Churches in the mass communications office. That was fascinating and offered me a glimpse of what I might do with my life. It was clear that I had not abandoned the media altogether. I also witnessed what the Church could do in changing the world by advocating for peace with focus, will, and decent finances.

Death Confronts Me

Returning to Boston in September 1972, I re-entered Boston University School of Theology. I knew I needed to hone my skills as a minister, so I enrolled in the Clinical Pastoral Education (CPE) at Massachusetts General Hospital, where I was cajoled and challenged, tested and failed. I tried and occasionally succeeded as a hospital chaplain. During that year, I also squeezed in and out of many identities, but found myself emotionally and spiritually conflicted in my encounters with authority, the sick, family and friends, so I entered psychotherapy. I began the work feeling undue pressure about my professional and personal identity issues, responding to the deep internal need for authenticity in my life and ministry. The therapeutic process lasted for more than three decades, on and off.

The internal conflict that launched my entrance into therapy began with my very first encounter with a hospital patient. When I entered her room, she took one look at me and shrieked nonstop for ten minutes. I ran away. After my first meeting with my supervisor I was directed to return and try again. This time I introduced myself as a student chaplain and asked if there was anything I could do. Her response—shrieking again. And yes, again I fled. Now that all my defenses were shattered, I returned a third time, and she shrieked as I sat next to her bed with tears rolling down my face for the helplessness of it. Gradually she became still and said nothing. After a pro-

Chaplain Ted Karpf before heading out to the floor at Massachusetts General Hospital, October 1972.

longed silence, I announced my departure, and only then did she inform me, "Come back tomorrow. I just found out that I am dying."

Facing Denial

I should have kept still and simply nodded. But anxious to please and make everything that was amiss all right, I tried to reassure her, breaking every rule of care and chaplaincy, and clearly making a fool of myself, because she was—in fact—dying. Over the next months, she taught me something about living and how to die, and I learned how to be "present" to another, especially her. Betty was a contractor violinist, often working with the Boston Symphony Orchestra. Only weeks before she had been playing concerts. "I was at the Stop & Shop [a regional supermarket chain] late one evening after a concert and stumbled over a box or something in the aisle. It was stupid, really. I was very sore for days afterward, so I went to the doctor. After checking me over—it was now more than a month since my fall—I couldn't even play a concert. My coordination was off and it was so painful to sit. The doctor advised that I should check with a surgeon. It was clear that I had done something to my body. I was stunned."

It took a while longer to schedule the surgery and face the possible recovery outcomes. But the surgeon's scalpel quickly revealed that her body was riddled with bone cancer and that she was in the last stages of her life. "I haven't known what to do. I am an only child and a single woman. When you showed up my door that day, you were the first to see how I felt, not knowing anything of what I had been told." Now in her late 50s, she had no one to call family, but I was there for the moment.

Facing the mortality of someone I knew only as a visitor and as a minister, I realized that I had all kinds of issues about death and dying. I was struggling with the finality and hopelessness of it. Sitting with her one afternoon, not long after our first encounter, I said, "I really don't know what to tell you in this situation. I am probably the worst person to talk to because I have no real experience and no real understanding of what it means."

She laughed, "Does anyone have real experience of their death and live to tell it?" I sat there somewhat dazed by her response and my obvious naïveté. Then she added, "Only your faith, as a Christian, has the audacity to suggest that someone who has died, and has been to hell and back, has returned to tell about it. What does that say to you, Ted?"

"Oh yeah," I said. "I guess you are telling me to remember what I know and to tell you what it means to me so you can tell me what it means to you." In that moment I discovered what it means to be "real" with another and particularly with myself, allowing myself to be utterly helpless, often without answers. She had called out my sense of loss and my inability to be in control of my fear.

Throughout her journey to death, it was essential for us both to find a way that she could come to a place of peace and if possible, me with her. We did. The day before she died, I asked her, "What would be the last or most important thing you could say or do?"

She quickly replied, "I want to play the violin one more time."

In extreme pain and with sheer physical agony, she did and did so with a curious, otherworldly smile. As she played we both wept, me for the loss I was now going to have to feel, and her for the end of life as she knew it. The next day she died. I was somehow resolved that it was all right. Betty gave me the legacy of being a human being. I owe her much. Part of the unwritten preparation for facing the onslaught of HIV/AIDS deaths was realizing that everyone will die in the way that they have chosen, often consistent with the way they had lived. Every death is holy. And even when there is little that anyone can do to alter the circumstances or situation of a death, a death with dignity is usually within reach.

Acknowledging Mother

I cannot continue this tale of calling without citing another crucial character. That would be my mother, Joan Shepherd Karpf. She practiced nursing professionally from ages 20 to 84. From my earliest memory, her concern for the dying and issues about the end of life dominated her conversation and her approach to caregiving for her patients. Much of her professional outrage stemmed from the fact that the will of the dying for the end of their lives was overridden by the professional medical community. "I can't believe that they would deny someone the knowledge of their own death," she said. "These people are being compromised or totally ignored by medical professionals. It's wrong. At least I can listen to my patients." When hospice appeared in America, my mother was among its earliest adherents and advocates. When I told her that I was entering the Church to do the work of the Church, although unhappy with my vocational choice, she reminded me, "You can't be a minister without caring for the dying."

I confess it was not something that I looked for, but it is now evident that her pronouncement and perhaps prophecy steered me in that direction, though I am just coming to understand that now. By age 28 I was helping to organize the first hospice—Ann's Haven—in Denton County, Texas, while serving as chaplain at the University of North Texas in 1976, having graduated from BU and being ordained an elder in the United Methodist Church the year before. Those lessons about death and dying were my mother's practice to the end of her own life. She was determined to die with dignity and respect. I became her fierce advocate and challenger within the healthcare system around the issues of death and dying, as well as effective healthcare for all. My mother's advocacy and determination are an unmistakable part of my own life agenda and calling.

Through the therapeutic process undertaken during my seminary career I learned that I had something akin to a vocation. Namely, that I was convinced of and convicted about my sense that I belonged in ministry. I just couldn't figure out how, much less where to make it happen. These first lessons have been tried, tested, defended, accepted, and rejected, both by me and institutions in which I have served. But the deepest truth is that my sense of vocation, that of being called, has deepened and expanded over the course of a lifetime. More than 40 years after entering seminary, I returned to Boston University School of Theology from 2011 to 2014, serving on the adjunct faculty as an instructor in religion, international development and public health. It was a first for me and a first for the university. Students from theology, social work, public health, and medicine registered for the course, offered three times. It was both interdisciplinary and unequivocally about "decent care": the concept I had developed at WHO as a synthesis of what we learned from the AIDS pandemic and what could easily be applied to healthcare in all situations. There, I was finally in a place where I could both give witness to what I had seen and also help in shaping the formation of those who were actively assessing their own sense of calling to ministry and service. There, I could begin the process of "payback" by raising funds— nearly $20 million—for the school to ensure another generation of education and excellence. There, I could begin the process of synthesizing the experience and wisdom of living a life by reflecting upon it and testing the stories and experiences daily with a group of youthful, eager minds.

Showing Up and Saying "Yes"

Calling is irrevocable, though God seems to maintain an open posture toward our personal and unlimited freedom, always and forever. I have often tried to make other choices and expressions, and yet always ended up becoming the priest in the most public of ways. At WHO, daily wearing a jacket and tie as a diplomat, after about a year the Muslim staffers began calling me "Father" or "Abba" as a sign of respect, after hearing from others that I was a priest. The Christians later followed the same practice, though I never wore a collar nor acted any differently than I usually did. Calling is about the steadfastness of love and acceptance over the long haul. Sometimes I get it right and at times, many times, I don't. Calling is about becoming ever more transparent and living into fundamental or core values which can motivate, enervate, animate, and maintain life. Calling is about faithfulness over all of one's life, while commitment is about showing up over and over and over again until I get it right and then … showing up again. Calling has become crucial to understanding my own identity. Without a sense of what it is to be about in life, I am simply set adrift in a sea of amusement and confusion. Everything is important and everything is equally unimportant, because nothing seems to be important without this sense of calling.

There it is again, the world's deepest need and my deepest joy, intersecting at the place where I am called to live. It seems impossible for me to live or enter my life without sensing why and how to be there. But maybe that is the mystery of what it means to live alive.

VII

Resilience and Resolve

I often want to say to people, "You have neat, tight expectations of what life ought to give you, but you won't get it. This isn't what life does. Life does not accommodate you; it shatters you. Every seed destroys its container, or else there would be no fruition." But some wouldn't hear, and some would shatter themselves on principle.
—Florida Scott-Maxwell, *The Measure of My Days*

"Teddy, my hope and prayer for you and for us is that a day will come when someone who comes to do good can be trusted for that alone."

My tears, until then falling slowly down my cheeks while I explained my forced departure from South Africa, were now flowing like a spring-melt river. As Desmond (Mpilo Tutu) sat extending his arms to me, I found myself reaching in turn for his warm and trusted embrace. His quiet presence steadied me for the moment, but then he curiously erupted in a giggle which melted into laughter. Almost as quickly, a long silence ensued. Then he spoke again. "Listen. I, too, yearn for a day when good men can be trusted to be good men, but my people are deeply wounded and will require time to learn trust and goodness. But Teddy, you must know that you have brought goodness and been a good example of selflessness and service for the people. You must continue this work, no matter where you are. God needs it and expects it from you." A few more moments of silence passed between us. I left the office, emerging into the radiantly warm South African spring light and resting my tear-stained gaze upon Table Mountain, in whose shelter I had—for but a moment—found "home" in Cape Town.

I guess I am used to change in all the radical ways. Resilience to me is the ability to work with adversity in such a way that one comes through it minimally harmed at worst, or even better for the experience. It means facing life's difficulties with courage and patience—refusing to give up. It is the quality of character that allows a person or group of people to rebound from misfortune, hardship, and trauma—and rebound I had to. The notion of resilience appears to be rooted in a tenacity of spirit—a determination to embrace all that makes life worth living, even in the face of overwhelming odds. When I have a clear sense of who I am and what my purpose is, I am more resilient because I am transfixed by my vision for a better future. Resilience is lived out in community; that is, we gather energy and tenacity from relationships that allow us to lean on each other for support.

What led to my encounter with this Nobel Peace Prize Laureate was simple. "Arch," as he was known locally, had become my spiritual guide and mentor in 2001–2004, during my time working in South Africa. We had first met 17 years before during his global activation of the faith communities of the world to assist him in the Anti-Apartheid Movement in South Africa. I was now in South Africa to develop an HIV/AIDS response within the (Anglican) Church of the Province of Southern Africa (CPSA), which includes the countries of Namibia, Angola, South Africa, Lesotho, Swaziland, and Mozambique. I would also do similar work in Zambia, Zimbabwe, and Botswana, as well as in Kenya and Tanzania, Uganda and Zanzibar, so it was really ministry within the southern quadrant of the African continent. I had been recruited three years earlier (in 2000) by the reigning archbishop, the Most Rev. Njongonkulu "Winston" Ndungane, successor and former chief of staff to Arch. Like so many, Winston was a victim of "the struggle" in more ways than I can name. He simply decided one day that my time in South Africa had ended, but the way he went about it was brutal.

Over the first five months of 2003, the bishop of Washington, the Right Rev. John B. Chane, the General Secretary of Anglican Consultative Council, the Rev. Canon John Peterson; and I had ongoing conversations about expanding the HIV/AIDS ministry to a global level, with me leaving South Africa about a year sooner than planned. However, in their reaching out for other partners, they had determined that I was "expendable." Because I had indigenized—that is, staffed the Office of

Gathered for the Anglican Primates Meeting in March 2003 (left to right): Archbishop of Canterbury, the Most Rev. Rowan W. Williams; the Archbishop of Cape Town, the Most Rev. Njongonkulu "Winston" Ndungane; The Rev. Canon Ted Karpf, Provincial Canon for HIV/AIDS, Church of the Province of Southern Africa (official photograph, Anglican Primates Meeting, Anglican Communion, Gremado, Brazil).

HIV/AIDS at Bishopscourt, the home and offices of the archbishop of Cape Town, by, with, and for South Africans—and had established the 23 diocesan bishops as chief administrators of the local funds for AIDS, I was no longer essential to the process. As I originally understood it, I was being called upon to replicate this same work across the Anglican Communion, particularly on the African sub-continent. While it appeared that my grant from USAID had been withdrawn by the funder, I learned later that it curiously had been re-assigned to be administered through Bishop Chane and Canon Peterson who were now free of any prior contractual restraints as they informed London in August of 2003. As a result it became necessary to remove me from the formula.

I suspect Ndungane went along with this because in addition to the millions of pounds already guaranteed by the U.K. government, there was the promise of several new sources of funding from the United States, including a private foundation and new resources from the President's Emergency Plan for AIDS Relief (PEPFAR). It appeared to be less about the work in the Church and more about the opportunities for enhanced benefits from the promise of newly acquired resources. I understood this because I had witnessed the innumerable opportunities for graft and corruption across the system inside the churches, particularly in the developing world. For example, the grant from the U.K.'s Department for International Development (DFID) was four times larger than the annual budget of the entire Church of the Province of Southern Africa (CPSA).

This first-ever grant to a faith-based organization in sub-Saharan Africa in response to the AIDS pandemic became the largest faith-based program in the world. It was an outgrowth of my work, during which I visited all of the dioceses of the CPSA in six nations and worked to establish goals and priorities toward building an effective, locally based response to the challenges posed by HIV/AIDS. This had been accomplished through a series of consecutive workshops conducted over a year in all 23 dioceses. I had also traveled to the United States and twice to London to raise significant funds from anyone who would listen to the plight of the Southern African people, particularly those living at "ground zero" of the global HIV/AIDS pandemic.

In a passionate presentation before Gordon Brown, chancellor of the Exchequer, on World AIDS Day 2001, I explained the challenges and opportunities of direct support to the churches of Southern Africa which, after all, were on the front line of the epidemic's impact. Late in 2002, I was requested to present a grant application, which was written in less than a month in round-the-clock meetings with the Christian Aid organization in London. I then journeyed to the United Kingdom Embassy in Pretoria, the capital of South Africa. An embassy-approved application was then forwarded to the DFID main offices in London. It was successfully funded three months later, and consequently brought £2 million ($3,200,000) from the DFID to support the CPSA HIV/AIDS program, beginning in June 2003, for up to a decade, eventually totaling more than £20 million. That commitment was the largest ever to be funded to a faith-based organization for HIV/AIDS. The CPSA Strategic Plan, which I planned, wrote, and worked through in each of the 23 dioceses, was the means by which autonomous self-management could be launched at the local level in response to the AIDS pandemic. Experts predicted the disease would kill up to seven million people within a decade in the CPSA region alone. Funding began in April 2003 under the auspices of Christian AIDS. As I look back over this startling turn of events, I had to ask myself, "How did I get to South Africa and how did I connect the dots which led to the funding from the U.K. government?"

White House Meeting

I had come to South Africa at Archbishop Ndungane's specific request to Bill Clinton at the end of his second term as president of the United States. The archbishop was a guest of the president at the 2000

President Bill Clinton shakes the hand of the Rev. Ted Karpf, executive director of the National Episcopal AIDS Coalition, while Deputy National AIDS Policy Director Warren W. "Buck" Buckingham looks on, at the White House gathering of faith leaders on World AIDS Day, December 1, 1993 (official White House photograph).

World AIDS Day observance at the White House on December 1. At a White House breakfast attended by South African Ambassador Sheila Sisulu, Sandra "Sandy" Thurman, White House National AIDS Policy director, reported that the archbishop apparently took President Clinton up on his offer to assist Southern Africa to meet the HIV/AIDS challenge.

The president is said to have remarked, "Anything we can do to provide technical assistance, we will do it."

To which the archbishop immediately responded, "You have a priest here in Washington, Canon Ted Karpf, whom I want to join me in helping us in South Africa."

Sandy then said, "That's Father Karpf."

To which the President added, "That's excellent."

I had provided counseling and chaplaincy services to Sandy's office and other White House staff for the previous five years and was called on by staff for counseling, prayers, and support. Archbishop Ndungane had known me and my work for some years beginning with the struggle

After-hours tour of the West Wing, 1995. In the White House Press Room are the Rev. Ted Karpf, David Karpf, and national AIDS policy director, the Honorable Sandra Thurman.

to end apartheid in South Africa in 1986. I had also attended Archbishop Desmond's retirement in 1996 as part of a delegation from the Episcopal Church in the United States. Although Archbishop Ndungane seemed to be taken a bit off balance, he was delighted when the president told him, "Well, in that case, you can tell Ted that he is moving to South Africa."

My participation was funded through a massive application for funds by the last USAID grant for faith-based activities in HIV/AIDS authorized by the Clinton Administration. After months of delay, though, the program became the first initiative of the newly arrived Bush Administration in 2001, falling under the banner of a faith-based initiative. The grant and many others for AIDS services would later morph into PEPFAR (the President's Emergency Plan for AIDS Relief), one of the largest HIV/AIDS programs in the world. But I am getting ahead of myself.

Canterbury, Cape Town and Dallas

In 2002, the year before the award from the British government, I was impatient with the British: their clear familiarity with and awareness of the dire nature of things in Africa, combined with the glacial slowness by which their remarkable response ultimately came, had the effect of slowing both my work and that of the Church to a near standstill. My impatience and frustration became well known after I challenged the archbishop of Canterbury, the Most Rev. George L. Carey, telling him that he should come up with a significant gift to assist the failing African churches in responding to the overwhelming impact of HIV/AIDS. He had offered a check for a few thousand pounds sterling (£3,000), indicating that this was all the Church of England could afford. I looked at his surroundings and quickly responded, "You might want to consider selling this property, Lambeth Palace. After all, it's so close to Parliament and its buildings at Westminster, don't you think that it might be worth something?" I was immediately chastised by the archbishop for my brashness and 24 hours later by my boss, Archbishop Ndungane. Even though I returned with the check for £3,000, my arrival was preceded by what was described by His Grace, Njongonkulu, as a "rather intense" telephone conversation with Canterbury. However, Lord Carey and I became respected colleagues of one another over the next several years as he facilitated a grant from the U.K. government to support—on a massive scale—the developing program in Southern Africa. Additionally, the archbishop preached about my AIDS work in Dallas and in Africa in his last three public addresses before stepping down from his position. While I was clearly cheeky and paid for that in Africa, the message of urgency about the African situation got through.

After nearly two decades in HIV/AIDS work, the chastisement from the archbishop of Canterbury, while significant and perhaps well-deserved for my cheekiness, did not cause me to be frightened or insecure. I had learned new ways to react to the potential of rejection or

Strategic planning in Southern Africa. Provincial Canon for HIV/AIDS Ted Karpf describes the way forward, Maputo, Lesotho, 2001.

controversy. I welcomed it in some dark way as another example to prove the corruptibility of institutions and their lack of good faith. I also even learned to see such moments as signs of hope.

Gay, Straight and a New Life

After leaving St. Thomas in 1988, I came out officially as a gay man. The Church had been anything but kind to me. I quietly stepped down when it was evident that my gay self had overtaken my straight self in my advocacy of gay rights and human rights. My gay self had overtaken my soul when repeatedly pronouncing Last Rites over dying gay men who were disenfranchised even in their dying, largely because of their apparent orientation and, of course, their illness due to AIDS. They were often desperately alone, in that their families rarely would attend them in life or at the time of their death. Overtaken when my personal passions and obvious attraction for a man caused me to divorce my wife and leave the raising of a family. Overtaken when deep inside of me I found myself screaming for acceptance while pronouncing acceptance for others. I had thought I had been careful not to do anything that caused anyone to believe I was gay. I did nothing to call attention to my orientation. My marriage ended when I separated from Kaye and the children in September 1988—after 13 years—and immediately moved in with Buck, who had been recently treated for an opportunistic infection and was subsequently diagnosed with HIV/AIDS. Through our acquaintance and obvious attraction, I fell in love with him. Our passion, coherence, and obvious affinities seemed predestined. Our mothers had even grown up in the same suburb of Boston and went to the same schools, though neither knew the other. His diagnosis led to rapid action and a decision on my part. Even if this was the end of his life, I was not going to run away or hide out. I wanted desperately to be with him to ensure his safe and secure passage. I can recall our first morning together. I felt that life was finally all as it should be. I felt that I was gender-consistent, body-compatible, and psychically balanced for the first time in my life. I thought, *This is where I should have always been.* The price, however, was high.

The presiding bishop of the Episcopal Church, who was sympathetic to my situation, called me to a face-to-face meeting in his office in New York in October 1988. The Most Rev. Edmond L. Browning—who years before had declared that there will be "no outcasts from this church"—welcomed me to tell him my story of loss and change, of incompatibilities between the Church's teaching and practice, of my fears and the risks of reprisal from the Diocese of Dallas. He admonished me that I must officially come out to the bishop of Dallas, Donis Dean Patterson, who had already made it patently clear that he would not countenance an out gay priest in his diocese. Browning had effectively asked me to act against my own interests, and I told him that there would be consequences for me. And there were.

After another called meeting, this time with the bishop of Dallas in the spring of 1989, I was immediately inhibited—that is, prevented from the practice of ministry—and then effectively excommunicated in the Diocese of Dallas or any diocese contiguous with Dallas for "conduct unbecoming a priest of the Church." When I countered with the threat of a legal battle through Church courts, there were consequences again. National Episcopal Church leaders residing in Dallas telephoned me, stressing concern, particularly for the state of the whole Church, and threatening me. I was cajoled, harassed, challenged, and charged by them with everything from the destruction of life as we know it to the downfall of the Church if I insisted on acting on my constitutional and canonical rights.

Finally, in the fall of 1989, the lawyer for the presiding bishop along with the Church chancellor, Mr. David Booth Beers of Washington, D.C., were deployed to meet with me and explain my position and the fallout that it would legitimately engender across the whole Church. This would be the outcome of my demand for maintaining and defending my legal rights to remain as a functioning priest of the church. This kind of meeting, I have subsequently learned, is rare, and such personal attention to the issue of one priest is uncommon. I had been, according to the presiding bishop's staff, a bit of a poster boy for the AIDS ministry in the Episcopal Church, nationally and internationally. In our meeting, David insisted that I must "get my file off the bishop's desk in Dallas" and become "forgotten." When I countered that my life and career were compromised with this reduced and restricted status as a priest and that I was effectively being disallowed to make a living as a priest of the Church, he replied, "We'll find a way to support you from a distance. But you are correct; you will probably *not* be able to function as a priest again for a very long time." He further explained that a deal could be worked out whereby the inhibition—a legal act of a bishop—would be lifted. No, I would never be able to function as a priest in Dallas or receive communion from the hands of a priest in Dallas, but I was free to find a place to function elsewhere in the United States as a priest in good standing. However, any recommendation of support for me and the effectiveness of my ministry would not be forthcoming from Dallas, even to move away from Dallas. Thus, I was effectively being inhibited without comment. It meant death for my career as well as my soul.

Excommunication is like death for members of the liturgical churches—Orthodox, Roman Catholic, and Anglican. Without the ability to celebrate the mass on my own or have access to the Lord's Table, I believed I was being treated as a lesser being. Excommunication, an ancient tool of the Church to separate the notoriously sinful from the rest of the community, has rarely been used in the twentieth century. It was shocking to be subjected to it. He further indicated that the current unsettled nature of my status and next steps would make life disquieting and uncomfortable for the whole Episcopal Church, and that there was no doubt that I had ample reason to "go public" with this story of injustice and cruelty for merely coming out as a gay man. It was noted that St. Thomas had become a "beacon of hope" as a life-affirming congregation and a model for many congregations facing similar challenges. Browning had often spoken of it as the parish where there really were "no outcasts," but also the one in which he would be reluctant to be rector because of its many emotional and spiritual challenges. The chancellor added, "We are asking that you be voluntarily silent about your current clerical status and the reason for it before any and all media. Your story cannot and should not be told! It will compromise the leadership of the Church and put the whole Episcopal Church into disarray. Silence, Ted, silence. To this commitment you must be faithful all of your days as a priest." I have kept that commitment until now, five years after my formal retirement from active ministry, with this writing.

Importance of Obedience

A word here. For me, my commitment was and always has been a matter of obedience. The day I was ordained I swore allegiance to the faith universal, the Church universal, and the Episcopal Church that I would live in obedience to my bishop even in the face of contradiction and disagreement. I have repeatedly struggled to remain faithful and loyal to the bishop and to the institution, such as it is, and have functioned often as the loyal opposition. But I have remained obedient. When asked for my assent, in effect I was being silenced. I had no idea

Ordination to the priesthood. The Rev. Ted Karpf receives the Holy Bible from the hand of Bishop A. Donal Davies of the Diocese of Dallas on October 18, 1982.

what that would mean for the long haul, but I agreed to it. Now that I am retired, I am more comfortable in speaking of these things. The good news is that in the last three and a half decades the Church has moved forward on the rights, responsibilities, and effectiveness in ministry of women and sexual minorities, with its recognition and ordination of women and gay, lesbian, bisexual, and transgender persons. When long-time colleague and friend the Rev. Canon V. Gene Robinson was consecrated bishop in 2003, I felt the rising hope that excommunication and silencing would not ever be used for the punishment of persons for being themselves.

I was restored to the ranks of the leadership of the Church in 1998 when I was named deputy to the bishop of Washington, D.C., and a canon of Washington National Cathedral.

The ten years of silence had finally ended, but not without both a cost and a benefit. Through work in the federal government in the Public Health Service I came to a deeper understanding of what government could and could not do. I had to form a persona that reflected my calling in a more secular way, and had to conduct myself within the bounds of obedience and silence about what had happened and why. It was an emotionally painful time, but again, in prayer I had the challenge of learning to live in contradictions and turmoil with little recognition of what I was going through. I was curiously alone and yet surprisingly successful at whatever I put my hand to. In 2005, I was made Canon for Life in the Diocese of Washington (D.C.) for my leadership in service to God, to the Church, and to humanity, for my work in HIV/AIDS in Africa with the Church, and around the world with the World Health Organization (WHO). This was done by the same bishop who had undercut me in South Africa and cast me out on my own with an invitation to never return to Washington.

The journey from oblivion to public recognition was tiresome and irksome, frustrating and disheartening, and even, at times, rewarding. What followed in 1988–1998 were reasonable accommodations to an awkward situation. While being a priest, I could not effectively function where I had created a new home with my partner. I could practice some functions of the occupation for which I was trained, and thereby would do tasks associated with my prior work as a priest. I could lead, speak at, and host conferences, address this public health issue, and call for

The presiding bishop of the Episcopal Church, the Most Rev. Edmond Browning, flanked by Pamela Chinnis, president of the House of Deputies, and the Rev. Ted Karpf, executive director of the National Episcopal AIDS Coalition, on the AIDS Memorial Quilt displayed on the National Mall in Washington, D.C., October 1996.

compassion and justice, but could not say mass or consecrate bread and wine in Dallas or any diocese contiguous with Dallas. However, I was invited to preach and celebrate three or four times a year at St. Bede's in Santa Fe, New Mexico, some 900 miles away. Thus began my relationship with the place where I now live and the parish of which I am still a part.

After my resignation from St. Thomas in Dallas, I was recruited to the U.S. Public Health Service (USPHS) by the chief administrator of the Region VI Office, Dr. John M. Dyer. We met by happenstance as I stood waiting in the ticket line at Dallas Love Field airport as I was heading up to Minneapolis to do an HIV/AIDS consultation with the leadership at General Foods. John was standing in line behind me. I later learned that that he had been following my career in AIDS work through the local newspapers and wanted me to step into a newly created position as regional liaison specialist for HIV/AIDS. He contacted Surgeon

General C. Everett Koop, MD, and explained my work this way: "His community work has been to call people into awareness of both the magnitude and impact of the AIDS epidemic. In the Public Health Service, I expect him to convene a wide variety of community leaders, demonstrate collaboration with key community representatives, and coordinate the responses of federal public health service agencies and effective partners."

Dyer's argument apparently worked. He created the position and, while there was no budget for the program, I began my federal employment in April 1989 by giving testimony about HIV/AIDS as an "expert witness" before the Texas legislature. During the next half a year, I found myself becoming redefined by my new institution's frameworks: from an outspoken church official to being a government spokesperson; from being a local religious leader with a message about an epidemic to being a representative of the federal government, replete with all the gag lines, "I'm a Fed, I'm here to help you"; and from being locally focused on a specific community to having a constituency in five states.

Texas, Louisiana, Arkansas, Oklahoma, and New Mexico had five completely different public health systems with five completely different assumptions and ways of achieving goals and objectives. I changed uniforms from the traditional clerical blacks with white collar of a priest to that of a Public Health Service representative, featuring khakis, blue blazer, a button-down Oxford cloth shirt, and tie (usually red, white, and blue). While I looked different, I felt the same: There were people to serve and a cause to which I could rally others. My authority was derived from the work alone: that of producing results which enhanced and increased engagement by states and communities in responding to their local AIDS outbreak. I no longer could depend on my old role and sense of tradition, rather depending on literally earning my stripes daily.

Over the next three years (1989–1992), I learned by doing: practicing the art of influence over raw political or economic power; reckoning with the creative possibilities and stultifying demands associated with the federal grants process; stimulating a hunger to see and use such grants as effective tools to jump-start communities into action; creating new programs and responses; living with the horror of unanticipated outcomes; and giving witness to leveraging good results within closed systems through unremitting advocacy on federal lawmakers and bureaucrats—all in order to create better options for persons affected by disease.

This job restored me to a level of expertise and effectiveness where I could feel both satisfaction and delight at serving others. But I also found myself in the midst of constant compromise driven by what the government could not or would not do to help communities in desperate need. Although I was initially out of my league in the public health world, I learned my new discipline through my own disciplines of evangelism and service. My job was to encourage, cajole, invite, or tantalize communities and states to respond in a healthy way to the demands posed by AIDS and, where possible, encourage personal changes and healthier lifestyles for those at risk of infection. Sounded like evangelism to me. The downside was that while I had limited voice in secular public health circles, I was to be very silent because of the circumstances of my rank and role as a representative of the government. Rather than self-censoring,

Receiving Public Health Service Award from Assistant Secretary of Health Dr. James O. Mason at the Department of Health and Human Services, Washington, D.C., in May 1990 (official photograph, Department of Health and Human Services, Washington, D.C.).

I now represented aspects of a compromised Republican administration (George H. W. Bush, 1989–1993) in denial about AIDS, which did not fit with my worldview and sense of justice. While programs did expand the services eventually offered to people living with AIDS, through the Ryan White CARE Act, the response was more reactive than pro-active.

In early 1993, I left government service and returned to AIDS advocacy within the Episcopal Church—licensed in the Diocese of Washington—to function as supply priest, thus enabling me to preach and say mass occasionally for vacationing or ill clergy for the first time in five years, as well as directing a national AIDS advocacy organization within the Episcopal Church with the caveat of maintaining silence about the past. This time proved to be a test to assess whether I was responsible and faithful as a priest, and had reasonable skills and sensitivity to various situations and communities within the diocese.

Shortly after, I was asked to assist in a conflicted parish for a year, on the condition that I would leave discreetly at the end of my time there without stimulating any disloyalty between the rector and the parishioners who had been in conflict on several fronts. It was a ministry of visible invisibility. Silence, discretion, and absolute focus on the task at hand were required. I did manage to leave the parish nearly a year later without learning the names of most of the faithful attendees and without creating any personal relationships or loyalties with anyone there. The diocesan Deployment Office deemed it a success in discretion and a clear demonstration of my effectiveness as a priest. Only then was I licensed to serve regularly across the diocese, serving first at St. John's Lafayette Square, across from the White House, where I preached to three presidents on summer mornings from 1993 until 2001, and later at Washington National Cathedral, the diocesan cathedral. After several years, in 1999, I was elevated to a canonry as an official liaison between the Cathedral and diocese, and years later was made Canon for Life. The upshot was that, at last, I had a church home.

In 1993, my new role as the executive director of the National Episcopal AIDS Coalition (NEAC) allowed me to advocate to the government on behalf of the faith community and for people living with HIV/ AIDS, as well as advocate before the Church's official bodies for inclusive and caring responses to the epidemic now affecting all kinds of communities across the nation. The Episcopal Church took national leadership in demonstrating to many denominations the efficacy of caregiving in the midst of AIDS. The Church now had a small army of volunteers, and it was my job to support them with education, information, national conferences, and opportunities to share their joy and grief in the work under the banner "Our Church Has AIDS." During the next five years, I was graced with public appearances at three of the Church's General Conventions (1991, 1994, 1997), along with NEAC Conferences in 1991, 1992, 1993, 1994, and 1996.

All the while I remained silent about what had happened in Dallas in September 1988. For all intents and purposes, by the official telling, I had simply sidestepped to the USPHS and then returned to Church work, as I was able to speak out and represent the Church in many secular and religious settings on HIV/AIDS. Two high-point moments occurred during this time: the joint consecration of the Lutheran presiding bishop at the National Cathedral where I functioned as chalicist (one who administers the chalice to those receiving Holy Communion) to the Episcopal and Lutheran bishops, feeling that at last I was restored to some semblance of my former role as a priest; and as an organizer and host for the celebration of the AIDS Memorial Quilt at the cathedral in 1996, during the quilt's display in Washington. As the director of NEAC, it was my role to host the NEAC Conference and to serve as the chaplain to the presiding bishop and host guide to the presiding bishop and president of the House of Deputies of the Episcopal Church while they were visiting the AIDS Memorial Quilt, which was spread out on the entire National Mall in Washington, D.C. I was also appointed the Sunday morning preacher at Washington National Cathedral's principal service, and later that day the host of the interfaith service at the cathedral, after the final closing of the quilt on the Mall.

The day of my preachment at the cathedral marked not only my restoration to the fullness of priesthood, but was a day promised long before by the late Dean Francis B. Sayre, Jr., who served from 1951 to 1978. My mother had had an encounter with Dean Sayre in 1956 while we were visiting the National Cathedral. It was during a family visit to Washington to see my aunt, my mother's sister, and her family; I was being scolded for moving through the barrier and climbing the steps of the great Canterbury Pulpit in a building completed only to the pulpit.

When she chided me for going up there, I replied, "I have to get used to it. Someday I am going to preach here."

My mother's response was quick and formidable, "That's not a reason. That's simply ridiculous."

Dean Sayre, passing by, overheard what was being said by this eight-

Appointed canon and installed in Canons Row, Washington National Cathedral, by Bishop Ronald H. Haines, October 14, 1999 (photograph by Ken Cobb).

year-old and the response of his agitated mother. He stopped, looked at me, smiled, and then said very gently, "Don't ever discourage a child's dreams. They often come true." Now, 40 years later, nearly to the day, it did.

By 1998 I was regularly preaching and celebrating mass at the cathedral and then was appointed, being a divorced, openly gay man, a deputy to the bishop of Washington for deployment and development. My letters of transfer from the Diocese of Dallas to the Diocese of Washington were completed by January 6, 1999. After 11 years, the ban on celebrating in Dallas or anywhere else was finally ended, yet I kept the silence about what happened and why for that entire time until now.

Cape Town to Geneva

So back to our beginning in Cape Town. It was September 2003. In July, the archbishop of Cape Town summoned me to his office to inform me that my work with the Church in Southern Africa had ended and that in late August he was appointing a local clergyman to run the newly funded program. He also suggested that the suddenness of this appointment was due to rumors of malfeasance in office, and the suspicion of possible embezzlement on my part. He then explained that I could not remain in South Africa as I would be forced to leave with the withdrawal of my work visa at the request of the Church. When I pressed further on the matter, he simply shrugged it off, saying, "It doesn't really matter what the reason. You are finished here." And with that I was dismissed.

During the subsequent meeting with Archbishop Emeritus Desmond, he carefully counseled me to write a letter outlining the record of my behavior, goals of management, and long-term commitments made by the province while serving the CPSA, thus clearing me of any malfeasance and clarifying my roles and responsibilities—which in all cases did *not* include managing cash resources of any kind—as well as a summary of accomplishments and achievements in office. There was an implicit but subtle suggestion that another agenda (not known then, but later revealed) may have led to my summary dismissal and departure from Cape Town. My letter concluded with a request that Archbishop

Ndungane corroborate my claims in writing, and that this document would be given to me during our exit interview a few days hence. It was. In that moment of thinking out and strategizing, I learned that Desmond Mpilo Tutu was a canny politician as well as a great spiritual leader and Nobel Laureate who reinforced in me the notion of speaking truth to power. Following the exit interview and receipt of the letter from Archbishop Ndungane, I left South Africa. This issue did not die, however.

Some 17 months later, in March of 2005, during an investigation by the Office of the Ombudsman of the World Health Organization (WHO), my employer in Geneva, the letter appeared again. Prompted by a complaint from a disgruntled WHO employee, based on the rumor that I was "booted out of South Africa for malfeasance and embezzlement," I was under investigation. The departure letter was used to affirm my innocence. I was to have been appointed to the *Corps Diplomatique* (Diplomatic Corps) of the WHO, a significant raise in pay and elevation of status as I had an interim appointment that began in late 2003.

The WHO–UN investigation included interviews and letters from all former employers and staff from the previous 35 years, as well as a list of character witnesses from the same period of time. I was also asked to respond in writing to a series of detailed questions, covering not only my time in South Africa with the Church of the Province of Southern Africa but the previous decades of my career in the Episcopal Church in the United States. As the WHO ombudsman observed, never had he seen "such a compelling lineup of witnesses," including Archbishop Tutu, or a track record "so publicly accountable." I was subjected to a three-month, unpaid suspension, which I took in the United States living with friends. Eventually, I was officially summoned back to Geneva. After a very costly UN-sponsored investigation, I was found innocent and absolved of all alleged infractions, all of which were outlined and addressed perfectly for the lies they were in the detailed separation letter from South Africa. Thus I was cleared of any wrongdoing and appointed to the Corps Diplomatique by the director general of WHO. With my promotion to full staff after the interim appointment, my overall tenure serving the organization lasted seven years, until, at the end of 2010 I turned 62, the mandated age of retirement. The letter which Desmond had directed me to write became pivotal to my taking up a different international life. A decade after the investigation, at a meeting of faith leaders at the World Bank in July 2015, Dr. Jim Yong Kim, my former boss at WHO and now president of the World Bank Group, introduced me to an audience of more than 400 at a dinner, saying, "This man was both my mentor and spiritual guide at WHO and he still is today." I was surprised by this statement as I often argued with and challenged Jim through the rollout of "3 by 5," a program for obtaining treatment for three million of the estimated six million needing treatment for HIV/AIDS by the end of 2005. The program used community contacts and associations of people living with HIV/AIDS, fostered ties within faith communities across the spectrum of beliefs and practice, and built collaborations between national and local governments, nongovernmental organizations, and healthcare providers. We failed to reach the global goal in 2005, but managed to get it in place by 2006. WHO had changed the paradigm of treatment, making it accessible, cost-effective, and available on a mass scale, against all odds. It was a moment of nearly miraculous consequences in the developing world, especially in Africa.

Redemption Over Time

My life changed again in Geneva. I had left another front line of HIV/AIDS, this time in Africa, for a place so far behind the lines of the HIV/AIDS pandemic that even the smoke of the battle did not reach the crystalline view from my desk of Mont Blanc above Lake Geneva. More than 20 years had passed since my first encounter with Jerome and his subsequent death from which this radical new life had emerged out of passion, recovery, heartbreak, and betrayal.

It had been an extended season of loss. First, my partner—Buck— announced that our relationship was over in January 2000. He had found another person and chose to leave me. Months later, my boss, Bishop Haines, announced his need to retire due to his wife's health issues. This caused an abrupt end to my time as canon of the cathedral, five years earlier than our planned seven-year commitment to one another. It meant a separation from Washington National Cathedral, the church I had come to call home after leaving Dallas so broken only ten years before. In Southern Africa, I had been revived and renewed by the creativity and wonder of the South Africans and their fierce determination to live into a new order, forging new lives out from under the shadow of apartheid. I broke up with several gay male South Africans, whom I had come to love and cherish, always wondering *What would life have been like if...?* During that final departure, when I looked out over Table Bay as the plane lifted above the clouds, heading to London in September 2003, I wondered what would follow from here.

Resilience and Resolve

Resilience and resolve have often come to be construed as a matter of merely learning the artfulness of maintaining one's resolve while living into becoming resilient. I am deeply combative by nature. Some would say I was rather defensive. And perhaps I am. Resilience has come to mean that I have lived multiple lives of starting over again by the grace of God when the way forward was blocked or altered by forces greater than myself. In that new position, I have also learned that beginning anew without expectation or agenda is the way to build a resilient life. Resolve has been a matter of finding myself in a situation and remaining committed to doing what I said I would do; that is, of keeping my word. Resilience is having the courage and fortitude to do what I can where I can and as I can. Sometimes artfully, often doggedly. But living into the next challenge or contradiction in order to find life, and find it as life to the full, is the final goal.

VIII

Death and Life: Will the Circle Be Unbroken?

You remember the songs of heaven
Which you sang with childish voice.
Do you love the hymns they taught you,
Or are songs of earth your choice?

Will the circle be unbroken
By and by, by and by?
Is a better home awaiting
In the sky, in the sky?
—Ada R. Habershon, "Will the Circle Be
   Unbroken?"

I do not fear death nor does the reality of death animate me. I have not feared death for a very long time. Perhaps it was in my genes? In my upbringing? Perhaps it was the relentless nature of being thrust into the dying and deaths of others which has either desensitized or inured me to death and its consequences? Maybe it was the hundreds upon hundreds whose deaths I attended in the midst of the suffering and loss of so many due to HIV/AIDS? Maybe it was the hundreds of funerals preached or the wringing hands held in the face of the finality of death and loss? I don't really know. In those early years of being a priest and ministering to the dying I quickly gravitated to the material from the book of II Esdras in the Apocrypha of the Hebrew Bible. It is wisdom literature, written at a time of great chaos and disorder—a time given to speculation and dreams of a better day. The passage offers these insights about attempting to explain human tragedy or loss and, as you can expect, the answers are tentative and incomplete at best. But for me these words have been a comfort because they allow me *not* to know, but rather to struggle in trust, albeit incompletely:

Limitations of the human mind (II Esdras 4:1–11)

Then the angel that had been sent to me, whose name was Uriel, answered and said to me, "Your understanding has utterly failed regarding this world, and do you think you can comprehend the way of the Most High?"

Then I said, "Yes, my Lord."

And he replied to me, "I have been sent to show you three ways, and to put before you three problems. If you can solve one of them for me, then I will show you the way you desire to see, and will teach you why the heart is evil."

I said, "Speak, my Lord."

And he said to me, "Go, weigh for me a pound of fire, or measure for me a blast of wind, or call back for me the day that is past."

I answered and said, "Who of those that have been born can do that, that you should ask me about such things?"

And he said to me, "If I had asked you, 'How many dwellings are in the heart of the sea, or how many streams are at the source of the deep, or how many streams are above the firmament, or which are the exits of Hades, or which are the entrances of paradise?' perhaps you would have said to me, 'I never went down into the deep, nor as yet into Hades, neither did I ever ascend into heaven.'

"But now I have asked you only about fire and wind and yesterday—things that you are bound to have met and have experienced and from which you cannot be separated, and you have given me no answer about them."

He said to me, "If then you cannot understand the things with which you have grown up, how then can your mind comprehend the ways of the Most High? And how can one who is already worn out by the corrupt world understand incorruption?"

When I heard this, I fell on my face and said to him, "It would have been better for us not to have been born than to come here and live in ungodliness, and to suffer and not understand why."

Friend, Foe, Familiar

Somehow from my own beginnings, death and I have been colleagues, sojourners, and even, occasionally, friends, often without question or rationalization. I have never found myself asking *Why?* or *How?* or *To what end?* While I have thought much about the life after death, I still consider it God's business. Even the founder of Christianity, Jesus of Nazareth, says relatively little about the afterlife or resurrection, other than to model it. And even with that event he leaves us speculating, if we are given to that sort of thing. As to my own mortality or finality, it is omnipresent in the fact that I live with congestive heart failure, kidney and liver disease, and now, arthritis and neurological complications. Thus, for the past decade I have had to actually consider my death daily and to face my own questions: *What is death/my death?* and *What are its consequences?* This realization is now part of my waking existential makeup. But this reality tends to unfold itself to me in slow motion. For that I am even occasionally grateful. I actually get the time and opportunity to contemplate my own passing.

While I was in South Africa, my heart was invaded by an unseen predator, a virus that ever since has been relentlessly destroying the muscle of my heart in good seasons and bad. Regardless of stress levels, lifestyle, or attempts to minimize the impact of the living of my life upon my heart, the deterioration and destruction of my organ continues unabated. Silently, without interruption, bits of heart tissue are destroyed and rendered useless over time. It continues until the pacemaker, which keeps my heart beating, will no longer be able to overcome the limitations of a failing heart. Recent good news, though, from my physicians at Brigham and Women's Hospital in Boston have indicated that the advance has apparently slowed or been partly halted because of my living at high altitude and the resulting manufacture of more corpuscles to carry more oxygen to the heart. Who knew? Another surprise in this process.

There is a curious poetry in this "death in slow motion" that causes compromise and loss, sometimes imperceptibly, and then suddenly presents a concrete loss for which I am not prepared or immediately ready to surrender peaceably. Year after year, I find myself attempting to negotiate bargains about my degree of loss or compromise, as in *If I do this, may I have another year or two of this or that?* Such bargaining is rarely effective and often less than helpful, but these vain efforts tell me that for all of my readiness to live into or face my own death, I am not always prepared to give it (life) up quite yet! Neither am I willing to vainly hold on to life or make many more accommodations to disease. Every intervention is another opportunity to rehearse my sense of death and loss, well-being or woe.

I should have understood this from the "root dream" that came so long ago when I was wrestling with whether or how to live into or reject my clear sexual orientation. That dream enabled or propelled me to examine my willingness to face into what I perceived to be something akin to my Last Judgment. That is, a moment of reckoning with my life and death. It was no more fearful than viewing moments of scenes from my life and then facing a set of questions about regret or about my ability or willingness to accept my own death, and hearing my constant claim that "I am not ready yet because I want to see how the story unfolds for my family." Indeed! While feeling vital and able to accomplish whatever I set my mind to, I was turning 40. I found that I was not quite willing to let go of this life and the stories and moments that go with it. Now, though, my hesitancy is informed by the reality that when I am brought low from the lack of oxygen, too much fluid, feeling disabled, or am limited by lack of breath or lack of further will, I am absolutely ready to get it over with.

So much of this process of dying is caught up with my own ego-centricity around not wanting to be a burden to anyone. Beginning in my formative years, I found myself being sorry for being alive. It was literally beaten into me that neediness of any kind was a weakness and therefore was to be covered up or eradicated, but never acknowledged. With therapy I learned to differentiate between battering and love, but soon learned that giving seemed natural and curiously less costly to me than receiving. That's a hard pattern to break in spite of rich life experience in which receiving was the learning. Every time I find myself in need, I am overwhelmed by the warmth of response with which I have been tended and cared for. Nonetheless, the fear of being a burden has stubbornly remained my stumbling block. This, too, as I have come to see, is a more seductive form of denial. It somehow suggests that I can arrange to not be a burden in my dying … that I am actually in such control as to believe—falsely—that I should be able to "do death" by myself.

The hard truth of death and life, particularly for those of us born into relative privilege and living in a human community of relative acceptance, is that we cannot—generally—do it alone or do anything like dying alone! My wish to do this alone stems from the fear of being seen as needy or dependent in some way, though the realities of life indicate that we all are inherently dependent. The fear of being seen to be such, though, still appalls me, even though my rational mind knows that this is the human condition and that it is crucial to dying with dignity and self-respect. Such is the conundrum in which I find myself today and is, perhaps, a clue as to why I am still here, pondering what it means and why. I have had to learn to be valued for just being here and being alive. It runs counter to a larger cultural theme, however.

Being Valued

Living in and being part of the American capitalist system of economics has provided us with a curious escape. As an extension of the work of living and being productive, I have fallen prey to the false belief that when I am no longer producing, my usefulness/value to the larger human community has ceased. This lie could not be further from the truth. I, each of us, is needed to just "be" in our time and in our rightful place, so that others can see how to approach dying and death and practice acceptance or lose resistance to dying. While I know—from decades of teaching and preaching living—that I am valued by God merely because I exist and for no other reason, the industrial model has a siren call which insists that my productivity seems to be of more value than my being. What I produce by way of product, even if it is a preachment or lecture, somehow legitimizes my being, thus perversely causing me to imagine that I have earned the privilege of being allowed to breathe and take up my bit of life in my human space. Now put up that notion against the inevitability and obvious tyranny of death and see what you get!

Of course, the seduction of being productive seems more fitting and more like being really human and of being a person of value than merely being alive. I tend to scoff at being for being's sake, saying in the back of my mind that this is a post-productive state, and then generalizing about how we must all be human, which means being vulnerable and subject to death. Nonetheless, I am uttering denials under my breath for fear of being found out or being revealed.

But when all is said and done—judging from the way I live—I have trouble living in this notion of being for being's sake, which is clearly informed by faith and hard to see very clearly in the midst of experience. When left with just myself, alone, and clearly now losing the physical capacities for self-perpetuation, I encounter my fears, my needs, my losses, and my limits. It is not a pretty or comforting picture. So I find myself praying for a quick and speedy death. *The least I can do,* I mistakenly believe, *is to get out of the way,* indicating that I have difficulty in accepting a time of sheer uselessness to others and myself and, in some fashion, being utterly dependent on others for support.

As I sit here contemplating my own death, which is really never far away, I can only report that the stripping away of controls or supposed controls leaves me emotionally and spiritually incapacitated at the front end, though it can become revitalizing and renewing at the far end. Why? It has become a matter of clarifying my own values, which is why I have written this entire book. It is a matter of re-entering my own story of becoming worthy in my own eyes and sharing the journey so that others may know that they are not alone in their struggles and speculations. Writing to this issue of life and death is about finding and clarifying the inherent worth of one's own being in the very act of breathing and being who and whatever I am in the precious and irreplaceable moments I have remaining.

My need to tell this story is two-fold. First, to find out where I am in my own process. Being an extrovert, I find that nothing is truly real until I say it or at least write it out. Second, to write it out gives shape and meaning to friends, colleagues, collaborators, and particularly loved ones in a more accessible way than just "saying it" in a moment approaching my death. Indeed, there is an unmistakable quality of legacy in all of this work of writing and thinking and praying. Perhaps there is even a hint of immortality somewhere in there? I confess to the fact that this legacy dimension of the final journey is most important to me. I am often asking myself, *Am I living into the fullness of promises and assurances I have offered others in such times, and does it hold true for me?* For the most part the answer is *Yes,* but it doesn't come without a great deal of soul-wrenching self-examination and self-criticism, and finally acceptance of the deepest promises of the faith experience.

Is this then a journey to immortality or the "blessed assurance" of everlasting life? *Yes* and *No.* It is perhaps better said that this acute awareness and experience are actually about non-locality of consciousness; that is, consciousness beyond the physical or material realm wherein the mover and shaper of human life is near at hand, guiding and informing the sojourner, not so much as being but as consciousness. For me, it is not the gentle Jesus image that many of my Christian peers tend to think of as comforting and assuring; rather, it is the hard and determined Christ who, as consciousness, feeds my soul.

Life is not without intentionality. The universe in its vastness allows for our presence now and always, transformed, transfigured, transmuted into … the Mystery. Somehow this is enough for me to know peace and serenity. In the experience of being with the dying, I have observed multiple times over an unmistakable moment of falling into … what I have come to call "the arms of love." I saw it often in the faces of the dying in those final moments before they gave themselves over to death. I see it in glimpses of those who have so advanced in faith or age that they co-exist between this time and the time to come. I saw it in the face of my mother when she gave up the fight and finally let go of her fear of death. I saw it in the face in one of my closest and dearest friends, another mentor, and my adopted "godmother," Tenn, who in her last days, saw both her late husband and mother, thus allowing her to move toward the completion of her journey on this earth. The "arms of love" is what so many rely on and fall into at the last. All the fight, fright, frigidity, and fear drop away into a gentle, warm acceptance and an assurance that "all is well, and all will be well, and all manner of thing shall be well," clearly penned from the observations and words of Julian of Norwich. In her time (fourteenth century), Julian looked out on the burning yards of plague victims and also into the hearts of many fearful men and women of her day, who came seeking her counsel, and there saw visions of divine completion in the image of the nursemaid who sweeps us up when we fall, giving us the assurance that we are eternally embraced. Need we more to comfort us when the darkness falls and comfort flees?

Non-locality and Connectivity

For me, that rock bottom conviction begins in the fundamental understanding that we are not alone. Another has been there before us. We are not the first to know this grief and this loss, nor are we to be the last. That is the essential meaning of the story of the incarnation of God. Secondly, that hope is constituted by the notion that our consciousness is not limited to the cerebral cortex of our brains in this physical plane, but is, by its very nature, part and parcel of the construction of the universe. At the time of death, it is often said that "you can't take it with you." I would maintain that you can. You must. You must take your memories, dreams, reflections, and awarenesses of your life. They are somehow amalgamated into the mind and heart of what I choose to call God, and perhaps what others may choose to call higher power, the One, the All, the Mind or the Memory of God, or simply consciousness. Thus I have come to understand that at death, the final surrender of breath and being, each of us actually becomes *more fully* who and what we were intended to be: sacred experience/consciousness in the mind and heart of God. Given that, it is safe to say that each of us—regardless of what we say or think or how we have lived or believed—each of us is enveloped in unconditional love, no matter what we have done. We can now inhabit the place where our hearts have always lived, but now our consciousness is fully present and fully connected to all that is of value.

This notion fulfills an even grander vision. Stated simply, history cannot be completed until the hearts and minds and consciousness of all people are fully conjoined into one and then are returned or rejoined to the mind and heart of God. Only then can God become the God we claim as the God of all experience. And only then will God be the God in whom all experience, all of life—replete with wonder and shock, sorrow and delight, joy and despair—are ultimately united as one with the One. The comfort here is that it takes a while. In the meantime, we are given these moments to live in wonder, praise, and thanksgiving for every remarkable and unremarkable moment. We are also given this time for learning to cope with the hardships and contradictions that come from living. Only then, in the twinkling of an eye, the hope and possibility for completion and finale happen when all that is becomes one with the One.

A distinctive curiosity of our time—a time marked by extreme rationalism as well as extreme irrationality—which offers validation or evidence to those who see it that way, is that something of us continues after physical life. The multiplicity of reports of premonitions about death—pre-death, post-death, and returning-from-death experiences of patients in extreme medical situations, as well as stories from those who have had that momentary glimmer of otherness, or shall I call it "after-ness"—convinces me that the survival of our consciousness leads to an unmistakable affirmation that non-locality of consciousness is not only real but in fact consistent with the laws of the universe. There are simply too many witnesses who make this fact irrefutable. In many traditions there is the notion of the ancestors. This was particularly true in Africa, Asia, India, South America, and Ireland where I traveled or lived over the course of my life. What struck me was both the immediacy and accessibility of the ancestors, not as the dead, but as the very proactive living who interact with our daily lives. There is truth in their experience, I know.

Consider an encounter with Roy, who was well-known in the Dallas gay community in the late '70s and early '80s as a very accessible and sexually active man. A nonconformist in every way, his dying due to complications from HIV/AIDS was no different. In those last days, he cried, screamed, gasped and generally became very difficult for the nursing staff to care for. I was called in to try to help calm him. Upon my entering the room, with Roy obviously having hallucinations, he cussed a storm and then became silent. Finally recognizing me, he wept. We talked very quietly and it was then I informed him that I would be out of town for the next several days, on spiritual retreat at the Benedictine Abbey of Christ in the Desert in northern New Mexico, so I would administer Last Rites at this time. His response was astonishing, "That's OK Ted; I will see you there." With that I proceeded to anoint and pray over him for a safe and calm departure from this life; a life to which he had been insistently, feverishly, clinging. I left the next day for Santa Fe, and then on to the monastery. It was now two days after I saw him. With no phone connectivity, I was incommunicado for more than a week. But within that time, early one evening after dark, Roy came to me to assure me that he had made the transition and it was all right. We spoke of his life for a few moments and his willingness, finally, to let go of his earthly existence in order to enter the larger life before him. He laughed, and said, "First, I came to say 'goodbye and thank you.' Thank you. Second, to tell you that I have discovered that spectacle is one thing and intimacy another. For too long I traded one for the other, but now I can say, at last I am home." Then he was gone. I learned upon returning that Roy had died within the same timeframe of our conversation. Was it a vision or fantasy? Was it him? Yes, I know, there is truth in our experience.

I have also come to understand that there is little of which to be afraid when it comes to death, except the loss of what I have understood as my own being in the form with which I have become familiar. It is an odd business, truly, but from sojourning in the Now, I am slowly coming to accept that it is the very nature of our bodily existence to be pre-set for destruction and corruption; literally from the moment of our conception, the inevitability of our dying begins. Thus, to honor the benefits and vicissitudes of a life of growth and change, I must—by necessity—accept the proposition and the fact of non-locality or non-bodily presence of consciousness in order to complete the necessary tasks that life teaches for my ultimate purpose to have lived at all. In the end, it is the foundation or touchstone of all the great teachings, philosophies, and religions that the end of life is life itself. I need no further evidence.

The gift of the Christian tradition for me is that it encourages one to give up life to Life on the assurance that love conquers death—or non-being—and to the extent that we overcome our fear, it does, particularly as we are living it. The vision of wholeness and union often described as the Reign of God or Vision of God, and now supported by the notion of non-locality, is greater and even hinted at by the teachings and preachments of the Christian tradition. It is not a matter of heaven and hell, which was an ancient teaching of cultural mythology, even in the time of Jesus of Nazareth. Life overcomes death in a radical new form. Non-locality simply means that consciousness is not anatomically based; rather, consciousness precedes and extends beyond our physical reality. We need only apprehend the action of consciousness to understand it as non-locality. Even Jesus, through the imagery of the Ascension, is asserting that non-locality is the way forward into the ... Brahman ... Completion ... Enlightenment ... the Unknowable. The curious Christian doctrine of the Trinity—not really Biblical per se but essentially a tenet of the Christian tradition—is a strange but remarkable way to describe non-locality by positing states of being: Father, Son, and Holy Spirit. Does that make any more sense than stating that non-locality of consciousness is what happens after the fact of our physical passing?

How I Talk of Death

Christoph was my first and most unforgettable intern at the World Health Organization. Ours was, from the outset, a dynamic friendship of respect, mentorship, spiritual sojourning, and guidance. I gave him absolute hell throughout his first months at WHO. He was brilliant, educated, aware, cocky, privileged, multilingual, and if you asked him, he would tell you that he knew it all. Except that he didn't; he merely wanted to. Late in his internship, we sat over a savory meal. I listened carefully to his life story and then made several statements about what I saw in him and saw for him in his future. He was on his way to the London School of Economics for an advanced degree and would be moving into business from there. Which he did. But his soul had awakened during our time together and began doing different things inside than what he had so carefully planned for earlier in his life.

In fact, in the waning months before his wedding, where I would be the priest-officiate, we talked of those values with his bride-to-be Johanna, who I also came to love as deeply. They'd shared a spiritual awakening in these days of preparation, as well as an intimate awakening as a couple during the season (six months) of our regular Skype calls. Chris left his upwardly mobile position at an internationally known pharmaceutical company and became the director of a social business, a modestly profit-making organization, dedicated to maintaining and promulgating native German plants in yards and gardens across Germany. His equally bright and upwardly mobile friends at the wedding wondered if he had lost his mind, but I assured them that he hadn't. It was all part of the natural development of a soul. After some time of being married, Johanna became pregnant and they had a child. Her name: Ada.

But tragedy stuck. I can only tell the story in our letters exchanged during this crisis in their lives. (They have extended their permission for me to share them in this volume.)

Dearest Ted

Two weeks ago our sweet daughter, Ada, was born. After a wonderful pregnancy the birth was, as far as that is possible, also a precious and joyous event. Jo and our daughter were in best of health so the midwife and doctor allowed us to go home directly without a night in the hospital.

Escorting Johanna Falk and Christoph Seifert just before their wedding in Berlin, 2012.

34 hours after her birth, Ada stopped breathing (the reason is still unclear). We called the ambulance, reanimated her in our hallway until the medics arrived who stabilized her. She is in intensive care ever since and breathes again, for which we are so, so grateful. Her reflexes and other functions returned excruciatingly slow which leads the doctors to believe in quite a massive brain damage. We are not so sure, however.

Since then life has been, well, completely different. The worst nightmare, a heaven of incredible support from our friends and families, who still carry us on many hands through this time and do everything for us that is possible and pray for Ada in every way they grew up with. We are experiencing shredded dreams and plans, arranging ourselves with a new reality that is completely uncertain—too much for such a short time but also something to grow upon.

Slowly we come to terms with parts of this and realize that Ada still lives and will continue to do so, that we will take her home again and start anew. And that a great part of our sadness is the loss of our expectations and plans, and that joy will return to our life again, only in a different form than expected.

There is so much more to say, but for now this must suffice. We have thought of you a lot in the past days and wanted you to know about this. Whenever we have the strength to send more, we will do so.

Christoph

Dear Johanna and Christoph

Your words to me this morning were shocking and overwhelming. I wept. Simply, there are no words adequate to enter the sacred space you now occupy. Your courage and trust, your real understanding and acceptance that life is different in the face of all these challenges is what I would have expected from you and for you. It is, indeed, the tenuous "first one step then another" journey which marks your faith and goodness. You do what you do as you do because you simply do it, and move with the tides and currents of living. There is a painful numbness of feeling at one level and a completely overwhelming sense of helplessness encompassing you at another. Bless you both for being the people you are and enduring life as it is—in the midst of a sea of sorrow co-mingled with questioning, rage, and fear—and yet still moving forward to embrace yet another day.

First I celebrate that for which I have been praying daily since the news in early springtime. Those first moments of birth must have been wonderful and stunning for you both. I can only imagine the fullness that it brought to each of you. I must say that I love the name Ada and actually have a good friend and scholar here in Boston who is an Ada: a great, strong, and thoughtful countenance and name. I am sure the families were ecstatic. That first day is indeed memorable and grounding. It is important to go back there often and harvest the joy that is there to plant seeds for the future.

In the next days, I cannot imagine the trauma: relief and shock that you have faced with these chances and changes. While there is no explanation for most of this, there is incredulity and confusion, doubt and grief: so much potential and possibility, so many dreams and hopes now altered by facts. Now you are in the midst of re-adjusting expectations and looking to the challenges ahead for the three of you. It is in every way a world of unknowns. I must now re-double my efforts holding you daily before the throne of grace and praying for the daily miracle of sheer wonder to enable you to return to your lives revived and afresh. The real wonder of life is how rarely it allows us to indulge our expectations, and calls us to make the walk daily into new possibilities in ways we cannot always know. It is a gift to be on the journey, but it is also a journey of faith. Knowledge or wisdom comes later.

It is obviously difficult to cast a future amidst so many unknowns, so you are left on your own devices to come up with a way forward each day replete with challenges. I would have to say, with the stunning support of family, friends, and loved ones, you will find a way that is more open or evident to either one of you alone. There is a distinctive community of love, support, and compassion surrounding you. I have seen it come to the fore in celebration and challenge. It will be there again, and I count myself as one of those who will find a way to stand with you. The great gift of your lives is that you bring people close to you who love you and will care for you. You have sown the seeds of love and loyalty very well.

Along these lines, where the daily challenges and choices really live is with each other. The force of a trauma such as this tends to be centrifugal—pulling you apart and separating in the most subtle and painful ways. But you have the chance to move closer together than you ever imagined, supporting each other in the unconditional love and care that you render your daughter.

Please do not forget each other and the unique wonder you each bring to the world and to each other. Strange as it may seem, you will need to love and honor each other better by paying closer attention and deepening your passion for and with each other. The care of your daughter will be enhanced and more alive if you are attuned and at ease with one another as you shoulder the burdens of the future by walking with her daily, fostering the love you both share for this new wonder in your lives. May she know that you are faithful, remarkable, and deeply caring parents who can and will defend, comfort, and shelter every moment of her life. That is who you are, and it can bring you together in ways you have not imagined and expected.

Finally, none of what follows will be done by you absolutely alone, as your families, friends, and loved ones will stand with you, alongside. But the truth of it is that you must bear these burdens, first and foremost, in the ways that you must do with each other, and at times, painfully alone. But there is more. The God who loves, weeps, and embraces us in joy and sorrow is eternally present, albeit in the thin and shadowy places between what is and what is to come. I hope you can trust that you will not be abandoned and that you are upheld in less apparent or visible ways. Therein is where this journey will inevitably go. Again, I offer myself as companion, sojourner, counsel, and questioner to go with you to the limits of my ability.

To say again I love you seems somehow so much less than what is needed or perhaps desired. But I do. I offer my daily intercession as means for you to know grace and mercy in the days, weeks, and months ahead. There may be a surprising grace which emerges from these challenges and heartbreaks. Time will be the teller and healer in all cases. I only know today that you are not alone. It is all that can actually be known.

Lovingly always
Ted+

Dear Ted,

Thank you for your words, they are comforting.

This morning, words fail me, for we have reached a state of utter hopelessness and grief. Ada has made some progress, but currently only barely escapes death when the nurses draw off her saliva. And there does not seem to be any fight in her against this asphyxiation. This might be her way of telling us to let her go?

On the good side: Jo and me are close and stabilise each other when one of us has a break-down. And all that keeps me going is the knowledge of her by my side.

Do you have time on the weekend for Skype? We are in need of help, because we do not know how to go through the days and weeks to come that will in some way or the other be so utterly painful that I simply lack the knowledge and fantasy how that can be possible to shoulder. Our emotions are beyond comprehension for us.

Christoph

Dear Johanna and Christoph

Once again, your words of despair over Ada's deteriorating condition broadcast through cyberspace to touch my heart as once again I am moved to tears. I am so sorry for all three of you, and yet strangely grateful that you have had these days to hold and care for her and give everything from your hearts and souls. What a gift of life you have given. In the mind and heart of God, there is a remarkable economy in which love and life given can neither be lost nor destroyed forever. In other words, you have given all to the life of this child and cannot be diminished for the giving. In fact, it comes back in surprising and life-giving ways.

As for Ada's condition, it is in every respect heart-wrenching and quite the challenge. This is known here as "failure to thrive." Nonetheless, this little one has given life her very best and had you there to receive what she could give and to support and sustain her—literally! Again, it is a gift of this life that you both have been called on to give everything without regard for the future, rather with joy and hope for her life in your hearts. So the notion of letting go is indeed a great agony, a deep sorrow, and may be a way of saying, "I love you enough not to compel you to suffer because of my sense of loss and sorrow." You may be asked to commit the most unselfish act a parent can give, to "let go."

It may come a time in which you are invited to do this and with it let go of the hopes and dream for her life. She may not be able to uphold those dreams in this life and may not be able to live into them. To let go is not an act of selfishness; it can become another, more challenging act of love: loving her enough to let her go on the journey she must make. I only offer this as a distant observer and someone who has unfortunately stood where you are standing more times than I can tell over the course of my life, and including in my own home as a young man. You will live through this is all I can say; and, that will you wax strong to become even more loving for another, should it be that way. If Ada cannot manage this life, then she may be saying to you, "It is time."

Your guilt is misplaced. You did nothing to be guilty. You are being invited to live and let live, to let go and let the future become what it will and bring an end to her struggle of suffering. The mystery of her life is caught up with the larger mystery of God and creation, of life and death. It is heartbreaking that we cannot save our children from the brokenness and incompletion of death. We don't always get to know how it happens and why it happens. We only know that we can survive and bring about life with new possibilities and wonders over time. I wish I could be with you to say again and again, "You are loved, you are accepted. This sorrow will last a nighttime and then give way to the inevitable morning." While the nighttime may seem endless, my beloveds, it is not eternal. Our faith knows this, and the experience of many before you can give witness to it, over and over again. It is about this trust that "letting go" calls us. Letting go means trusting God, trusting each other, and trusting life to be what it is.

I can only continue to hold you all in my prayers daily and through the nights ahead. If Ada is to complete her journey, then that is what we will come to accept. If she is not finished, we welcome her back into the journey to joy today. Not being physically close to you, I cannot hold you as I would like at this tender time. Please know however that I am holding you closely in my heart.

Lovingly always
Ted+

Dearest Ted,

A few days ago, we moved to a hospice with Ada. At first we were shocked and uncertain; now we know that it was the best best best thing to do. We are shown a way towards peace there and have many happy moments with Ada while we know, more than before, that she will die. When? We do not know. She has already lost weight and this is an indicator. Apart from that she seems to love the time with us as we do love her.

At the moment we are glad for the calmness and as much as our friends and family have visited us daily, we now do concentrate on Ada and rarely see anyone.

Just to let you know that we have come, physically and emotionally, to a much better place, and also that Ada will go. Our hopes have been destroyed, but we glimpse a ray of what else might come, what a gift our sweet daughter might have given us. Although I fear that I will never accept the price for that gift. That might be the challenge.

Do you remember the words we had chosen for our marriage:

Denn die Liebe ist das Band, das alles zusammenhält = For love is the bond that holds everything together. (Colossians 3:14)

We have thought so much about these words in the last week. All that we have done, all the little steps that have brought us from Ada's birth to the hospice, were taken because of love. And love will also be the bond to Ada after she has gone. We are glad to have chosen these words with you when planning our wedding.

Christoph

"For love is the bond that holds everything together." Reciting their vows, Johanna and Christoph, Father Ted presiding, Berlin, 2012.

Ted

Ada has passed away peacefully a few hours ago. We are sad, relieved, empty, so many things at once.

We have a few days to say goodbye, then all three of us will leave the hospice.

Thank you for your support and comforting words during the last 7 weeks. More lies ahead, but better times will come.

J&C

Dear Johanna and Christoph

Again the searing pain of loss is for me is untellable. Yet I am thunderstruck by the length of her days, the fight for life, and living of it to the full surrounded in love and compassion. She has experienced our best and takes that knowledge to the heart of God, where it informs and changes all of life from this day forward.

Her 50 days—her pentecost—allowed us to glimpse the wonder of love and the power of life, the pathos and joy co-mingled, which prepared us for her final ascent into the heart of and the mystery of God. I am grateful for her and deeply proud of your faithfulness and steadfastness with one another and with her. Ada will be remembered always, and the power of her life will bring new possibility in all that you say and do.

I grieve with you both in these days of sorrow, and hold you ever closer. I hope that your journey home will bring new hope for better days and that you will in this darkening time of the year find light and life. My love extends into yours. Thank you for letting me and so many others sojourn with you in this time. Let us talk soon as I will be leaving Boston in 10 days.

Lovingly always
Ted+

Dearest Ted,

Thank you for your words about Ada. It is a great comfort to know that you are with us. Much time has passed and many times I wanted to Skype and talk and write—but then all the exhaustion of 50 long days flooded over me while I started working again. Christmas came, Sandra and Peter from Cambridge came and stayed with us, and now the year is nearly over. May 2014 be a calm year!

Ada's funeral was a sad and joyous and powerful day. So many people, so much love. Even today, 18 days later, the flowers on her grave remain beautiful in the wet and cold air, and so many friends come to visit her that they run into each other.

For us, many challenges lie ahead. Most of all: accepting. Accepting that we are no longer responsible for her, that we cannot hold her anymore, that we are allowed to move on, that this has actually happened, is happening. We have great support from the hospice and also beyond. But the sheer size of it will take time and effort.

How are you faring in New Mexico? How is retirement treating you? Please let us know if you have good Skype access there. It would be so, so good to talk to you and to see you.

Lovingly,
Christoph

Dear Christoph

It's nearly five months since we last spoke. I have not heard from you and wondered, how is it going for you both? I hold you daily in prayer but have become anxious at hearing nothing. I am settling in New Mexico and into the wild West, but loving every moment.

Hope this brief now finds you well.

Lovingly always,
Ted+

Dear, dear Ted,

Five months already? Oh my. Not hearing, not knowing can be distressing, so please excuse us if we caused this.

Today it is 6 months exactly to the day since everything began. And today was the baptism of a dear friend's son, not an easy but also a beautiful and necessary day.

As I do not know where we left off: Ada died on the 28th of November and we had three days of mourning in the hospice with her where we could say goodbye in a very intimate and beautiful way. This is quite unusual in Germany today where normally the dead are ripped from you and brought to a cool place as soon as possible.

On the 10th of December we laid her to rest in an old cemetery that we love and where we used to go quite often for walks. Her grave has become a place of meeting and contemplation, it seems, because friends and family go there and on weekends sometimes meet each other.

The first days after her death were marked by grief and relief. Then came utter desperation and exhaustion. Johanna pulled herself together, got a little boost from finding a new job in parliament in February (she just said I should send you her dearest wishes) and then literally crashed two weeks ago. That Saturday has been the darkest moment of her life, I believe. Somehow we found a way out of the darkness, and this week something has released in her. Even though she is still so, so sad, it is a different sadness, one with less pressure, I guess.

My route was different. I never managed to pull myself together, so

December and January were awful and demanded all the strength I had
left. Through wonderful counseling I discovered another strength in me,
however, a more mature one. And it is with this strength that I rebuild
myself slowly. This has changed my attitude towards sadness to a more,
well, accepted sadness.

Accepting seems to be one of the big challenges in this. And how much
we have learned in this brief time, how it has changed our attitude to life!

How is your time next weekend? Skype? Jo and me would love to see
you (given our connection works) and to talk to you.

All our love
Christoph

This intimate exchange of hopes and fears, words and wishes, comforts
and sorrows says what it means to be in community and in communion
with those whom we love. I am pleased to report that Amelie was born
to Christoph and Johanna some seventeen months later and two years
later a son, Leo, was born.

Invitation to Life

The hard part of dying and death is the loss of and loss to family,
friends, loved ones, compatriots, and collaborators. We love others
because we are, by our nature, given to relationship and kinship. We
long for it, we search for it, we embrace it, and occasionally we reject it
for the burden it can be. But it is our nature to be connected to one
another. There are volumes of questions posed by men and women
across the ages, and the angst associated with those questions, which
fill thousands of libraries across the globe. Death is, after all, what we
most fear and most dread. There are also the volumes of devotional
material and assurances from all religions and philosophies about the
next steps. Thus, for those without clarity, or their own particular
answers, there is no lack of speculation available to all. Rather, it may
be helpful that in locating the final truth of our lives, it is that we must
work it out with whatever we possess: our experience, our reason, our
traditions, our speculations, and our hope. As for me, I live in this tentative faith in which I am learning to more gently hold life in my own
hands and yet keep my head and heart open to the wonder and awe
which the end of life inevitably brings. Even then, I have no idea what
actually happens when all that is within us becomes one with the One.
Clearly at that time, there will be more story to tell. Amen!

IX

Generativity: Parenting

We must recognize the claims of reality in us, even those of us who are venerable holy men or women. Scolding or excluding parts of ourselves or shutting the door will not do. We must admit what is there ... and must recognize, perhaps with awe, the intensity of the feeling of which we are capable, and try to meditate on its meaning. Only then can we begin to use all that emotion effectively. And so, in the same spirit, with the other presences, ignoble in fact or fancy. They are part of our lives, the way we really are and the way we must be willing to see ourselves.
—Ann and Barry Ulanov, *Primary Speech: A Psychology of Prayer*

"You know, Dad, you are many things, but the one thing I count on is that you are utterly consistent and you are constant. No matter what is happening and what it means, you can be counted on to be present, to show up, and to never stop loving us." David Warren, my son, said that when he was 19 years old after nearly two years in a halfway house for drug addiction. At more than 34 years of age, he is in his third or fourth recovery, this time after six months of incarceration for a probation violation and a number of DUIs (driving under the influence of drugs or alcohol), and yet he still expects the same dad to show up. And this dad does, not with the resources and rescue of yesteryear, but with full-hearted, unstinting acceptance for what is.

His sister, Deborah Michelle, some years earlier, when she was 34, reported it somewhat differently with these words: "Dad, you know I have listened to you my whole life, even when you thought I wasn't lis-

The thanksgiving walk after the implant of a pacemaker in 2006. In the south of France on the way to the Camino to Santiago, this time starting in Portugal, Ted and David Warren Karpf, May 2007.

tening. You have always been there for me and I count on you for thoughtful judgment, clear vision, and an open heart. I count on it, Dad. Don't change, ever."

Generativity, a term developed by the psychoanalyst Erik Erikson in the 1950s in a series of essays, and later formalized in *Identity and Life Cycle*, denotes "a concern for establishing and guiding the next generation." In his stages of psychosocial development, generativity is defined as a struggle against stagnation that ascends during adulthood. Generativity in the psychosocial sense refers to the concern for establishing and guiding the next generation and is said to stem from a sense of optimism about humanity. It can be defined as creativity between the generations. Generativity can be expressed in literally hundreds of ways: from raising a child to stopping a tradition of abuse; from writing a family history to starting a new organization. One can set out to make a difference with one's life, to give back, to take care of one's community and one's planet. Jonathan Zittrain defines the term more broadly: "Generativity is a system's capacity to produce unanticipated change through unfiltered contributions from broad and varied audiences."

I doubt that I could have achieved anything of lasting value in this life had I not learned to be a father to my children. Their births in my middle thirties led to a complete rethinking of my life and reshaping of my understanding of who I am and why. Even now I look at my son and daughter with deep admiration and gratitude for their willingness to educate me in the ways of being their father. So much of my life before them was rather self-centered and totally caught up in my struggles for identity and purpose, which was focused on mission to all others—though not necessarily family. All of this was definitely unresolved and exceedingly tentative, even at their respective births.

Learnings and Institutions

The lessons of the parenting experience are relatively simple. Generativity requires a willingness to make life better than it has been. It requires the investment and trust in tomorrow and a deep desire to improve the world, the community, the family. Constancy demands staying in the process, even when the price is excessive and goals seem to have gone off the tracks. It is in the essence of being human, I believe, that we will inevitably stumble, falter, fall, and fail ... often! But climbing back on the pony and seeing where it will go requires an indomitable spirit, a willingness to openly admit wrong or failure, and a strange adventuresome delight in starting over, again and again. David and Deborah have afforded me that rare opportunity to learn from them and with them. This learning has been crucial to the perfecting grace that has happened to my life. Without them, I would have been lost and more fearful than I usually am. Without them, I would not have had to reprioritize my life as often as I have. Without them, I would have been half a man, half a human, and half a priest. They taught me grace in the face of utter contradiction and frustration, and they taught me that love is forever and unconditional. Sometimes I actually live into truths and celebrate what is there.

Generativity is not only about parenting; it is fundamental to the way I have approached institutions and community. To be legitimate, institutions must reform themselves by re-inventing who and what they are in every age. I have found that my sole mission for life is to enter the dysfunction and, while there, aim to alter the realities of the institutions and their way of being. Over time, institutions seek to preserve themselves without considering their mission and purpose. In other words, they lose sight of their "why," and their "how" takes precedence over everything. It seems to be the way of things that when humans arrive at a good idea or an institutional solution to a nagging problem, we go to sleep and do not understand the need or necessity of revision or renewal. Yet in every age, needs change and new demands arise. Thus, just as in loving another person or as in any vital relationship, nothing can be taken for granted.

I had learned early in my training that I had difficulty with institutional life. Studying world religions from 1972 to 1974 with Dr. Daud Rahbar, professor of world religions at Boston University School of Theology, created an excitement and curiosity I hadn't expected. I am drawn to the wonder and mystery and ways of worship and devotion observed by much of the world, but Daud's ability to call his students into the dance of the spirit of all religion was truly a discovery. A Christian convert from Islam who hailed from India, he invited all of us novices to sit and chant and listen to music older than time. He was a rather skilled musician and cook, so dining with the Rahbars was as much about cooking the food and listening to Indian music as it was about the religion and culture. He seemed to understand the sheer majesty and wonder of the wisdom of the ages and shared it abundantly.

Over our time together he and I became rather close, which invited him to share stories of his own conversion to Christianity from Islam and the negative reaction of his religious experience as a Muslim growing up in India after partition. He told of the intolerances of "true believ-ers"—Christians and Muslims—in Cambridge and in India. Having a considerable amount to say about such believers, he warned me about the inherent prejudices of faith institutions and leaders, stating, "They are only interested in their power and control. While I am grateful for my faith in Christ, I cannot truly accept the structures of organized reli-gion without some regret. It only hurts to think about it to this day. I thought they would welcome a convert; instead they treated me as a second-class citizen." He went on, "I lost out from rejection by my family as well as from the Church believing I was not quite what they wanted." In that spirit he warned me, "Teddy, you are not meant to be in the heart to the Church and its power. You are a priest of the marketplace. You belong to the world more than the institution." I laughed it off, saying, "Daud, they would never have me in the seat of power. I find it so silly, with its need to protect itself and maintain control. They'd throw me out in a heartbeat."

This proved to be curiously predictive of my future. While I found myself an effective and functional "Number Two," both in the Diocese of Washington and the Church of the Province of Southern Africa, I could never accept being in that role as "home." This unease with the role did not preclude my love for the responsibility. However, I really couldn't accept the controversies associated with power: who had it, who wanted it, who needed it, and who rejected it. I found life at such a center often more repugnant to than desired, yet out in non–Church world, I was totally at home, always at ease. It is still that way. But the notion of generativity freed me to become more effective and thoughtful in my actions.

Renewal in my experience is the state of constancy for love. The way of expressing it may be constantly in flux and, because it is about growth, it should be. The same holds true for institutions and commu-nities. Only scrupulous vigilance about *what* is being done and *why* can ensure that one does not slip into lethargy and somnambulance (sleep-walking). Many institutions, especially the ones where I have spent most of my life—the Church and government—seem to lack such vigilance and thus emulate this disastrous model of dysfunction.

Generativity seems to suggest that it is our duty to renew and revive our communities and institutions from within. Many of the clashes I experienced have taken place on this plane of change. I am often abrasive in my unreserved and plain-spoken critique, which has managed to get me into trouble—professionally and personally—all of my life. My hope and desire are for nothing more than improvement and change, while my position is often perceived as outright faithlessness and acerbic hostility. This is where the role of mentor has become my best means for catalyzing change and fostering human development. Mentoring requires that I release my faithless ambitions, such as they are, and invest in the well-being and insightfulness of another. Mentoring has been about standing alongside, offering advice when requested, sharing insights when needed, and suggesting alternative views or realities. But not necessarily doing it myself or having it done my way. Stimulating trust from the other to expand my vision and their own to create something wholly new and perhaps utterly necessarily for the future is the more achievable goal and goes a long way to mitigating the impact of personal ambition. "Why was I there?" I often ask. Then I am forced to review the mandate and the mission and move from there.

Generativity and constancy are opportunities for grace and wonder. Walking daily by faith and experience, one learns to accept the integrity of the choices and responsibility and implications for personal action. Constancy suggests that one can and does remain true with personal integrity and self-respect for a lifetime. Living into faithfulness within institutions and communities requires an aesthetic boundary and purpose. Loving cannot be a matter of reciprocity, for it must be freely given without expectation of fulfillment or return. Loving each of my children for the unique human beings that they are has called me out of my self and my own painful past with its overlay of issues.

Being a father was one of the real surprises of my life. I just never expected that it would happen. It wasn't so much a matter of being a gay man, as much as feeling quite inadequate to parent anyone. Growing up in violence, abuse, and emotional instability left me deficient when it came to the notion of parenting. The awesome responsibility for the life of another seemed more than I could muster. Nonetheless, over nearly seven years of marriage, Kaye convinced me that my parenting skills, honed as being the "father" of a congregation, and family support skills were strong enough and appropriate enough for me to be a loving father. Deborah Michelle was born in March 1982, during spring break at the

Ted with David Warren (age 5) and Deborah Michelle (age 8) in Dallas, 1990.

University of North Texas, where I was serving as chaplain; David Warren arrived in 1985, during Easter Week, when I was serving as rector of St. Thomas the Apostle, Dallas. Both birth weeks are significant in that I was able to have the time off for assisting Kaye in the childbirth process and be totally engaged in the first blush of parenting, instead of attending to professional duties.

The pregnancies for each went well as we prepared our home to receive a child. Deborah was born as I was leaving the United Methodist Church and becoming an Episcopal priest. David was born during my first year as rector of St. Thomas, the epicenter of the AIDS epidemic in Dallas at that time. All that said, I still wasn't sure that I could be a decent parent. I had so little to go on as to when to hold on and when to let go. I attempted to do life and family differently from the home of my birth in that both children were utterly wanted, loved unconditionally, and given the best of whatever we had for them. Kaye and I were unstinting in our regard and support for these new people in our lives, sparing nothing. The outcomes have been surprising and wonderful, and at times, woeful and profoundly frustrating. Deborah at 37 is parent of her own firstborn little girl, Selene Ember Rose. She is married and a professional woman. David at 34 is still at home with his mother and stepfather. He struggles daily with his addictions to drugs and alcohol, holding the same kind of job he has held since he was 19 years of age, waiting tables, though more recently he was managing a restaurant and staff. Now he is awaiting the court's decision as to what his next steps will be, having fallen off the wagon again in 2018.

Genius and Consequence

Rather early, both my children demonstrated that they were precocious. Deborah was quite verbal and actually well-spoken by the time she was two-and-a-half years old. In fact, she knew the entire Mass by heart by the time she was three, echoing my words at the Sunday celebration, which always gave newcomers pause and the congregation sheer delight. By age four she was teaching other children in the nursery how to receive the bread and wine at Holy Communion, with these words, "the Body of Christ, the cookies of salvation"; "the Blood of Christ, the juice of joy." Improvising was always encouraged, but not usually at church. Nonetheless, her words stood.

David was an especially intelligent, talented, and gifted child. At only several days old he was pointing at everything he saw. By the time he was five months old, he was crawling. While naturally adventurous, he was also cautious; for instance, he would sit in front of a door, carefully observing its movement for an extended period of time before he would finally push it open to go through. We put him into Montessori School at a little over two years of age, in part because his mother said, "I can't keep up with him and his expanding interest in virtually everything." At first, he seemed to do well, but after several months, one of his teachers called us and asked for a meeting.

The teaching team was a bit flummoxed and began with, "Do you know what you have there with David?" We insisted that we did. They went on to explain that he was a genius and capable of a great deal. And while he had difficulty socializing with other kids in the classroom, he was really quite adept at many things far advanced for his age and experience, especially his comprehension of complex thoughts and actions. They asked us if we were willing to put him into a more advanced program for genius children. I retorted, "How is he relating to others again?" To which they responded that he had some difficulty. At that, his mother and I asked them work on the social aspect of his personal development, rather than the genius capacities, which we believed would not diminish.

In the next years, David demonstrated a tremendous aptitude for visual art. In Washington, D.C.'s National Gallery of Art one day, he wandered off and into a room to observe the work there. It was a retrospective of Pablo Picasso's work: 100 years of Picasso, all in one room. David commented, "Dad, it's about the form. Picasso is assembling and disassembling it, coloring it, and exploding it into its many parts; but all the while, keeping his understanding of the human form." He was maybe eight or nine years old at the time. I had no real response, other than, "Good observation." The museum guard was instantaneous in his response. "The kid's right. I've listened to and watched hundreds of people visit this room for the past several weeks and that kid gets it better than any of them. The kid's right."

David's favorite artist of that time was Henri Matisse. So when we came upon a number of Matisse collages and paintings, he was aglow. For the next days with us he made numerous collages after the style of Matisse and developed magic marker versions of the paintings he could recall. I still treasure his carefully crafted Matisse collage placemat for my dinner table.

David was not only interested in observing art, but in replicating it and creating it. At age four, he had mastered the stop button on the video player, enabling him to draw and paint the cartoon cells from the Disney movie *Aladdin*. These were not the typical childish pictures of a four year old. They were actual full color reproductions of the cartoon cell which he was observing on the TV screen. At eight, we had him enrolled in art lessons at the Houston Art Institute, and during his summer vacation period in Washington at age nine, he studied and practiced watercolor painting with a well-known local artist.

After two weeks, the artist came to us and said, "He's amazing. This kid has more talent in his little finger than I do. He should be teaching me. But he becomes really frustrated and impatient with himself and the time it takes to get the details of technique when it doesn't come easily to him. He is perhaps too young for learning watercolor technique, but his instincts are stunning. He becomes so impatient with himself that he becomes angry and gives up. But he is so talented. I hope he continues."

David took up drawing over the next several years. In fact, he still travels today with a small sketch pad and pencil in his back pocket, drawing what he sees with remarkable precision. At fifteen years of age he did a black-and-white pen-and-ink cartoon of me as a monk, using the pointillist technique. It is a *tour de force* and testament to both his concentration, attention to detail and his sense of artwork. I am proud of this creation by my very talented and gifted son.

David's introduction to the world of drugs began on a playground when he was eleven or twelve. As he told us years later, some older kid gave him a couple of tabs of LSD. Shortly thereafter he was diagnosed with ADHD, for which the doctors recommended Adderall, which is amphetamine, dextroamphetamine and mixed salts, to help him gain focus. For several years, both he and Deborah, who had exhibited signs of ADD, took this medication. David also was diagnosed with dyslexia, which explained why he was having trouble reading in middle school. By eighteen, he was able to read with a certain facility that was, in many respects, breathtaking for his achievement to automatically reverse what he was seeing. But that same mind was rapidly becoming clouded with drugs and alcohol.

Both children seemed to excel at school and in verbal and physical accomplishment. Both were avid horseback riders, each elegant in their riding. It was a privilege to watch them. Their straight backs and obvious control over the animal and yet the willingness to trust the horse and its gait was thrilling to me, who had only aspired to become a rider, but never really succeeded in maintaining the trust and rhythm with the animal. They were natural kids in so many ways, and delightfully intelligent and articulate.

While David left college after his first year, he returned later under his own steam to the University of Houston at 21. Having only a GED

David and Ted sailing with whales in Cape Bay, Cape Town, South Africa, 2001.

and no college entry exams, he took himself to the campus and without his mother's or my knowledge, went through a rather private admission process, which culminated in an interview with the dean of the College of Engineering. Apparently David impressed the admissions staff with his abilities in mathematics, which he had not studied in school since he was fifteen. When the dean interviewed him, he gave him a theoretical engineering problem that David did in his head while the dean spoke.

When the dean complimented him on his remarkable skill in physics, visualization and of understanding the problem, he added, "So David, you clearly got the right answer. How would you like to learn the formulae and methods which supported it?" Dave's response, "There are some?" He was that kind of kid. Talented, gifted, highly intelligent, and remarkably curious.

I have been learning over the years that this can be the very kind of kid who falls prey to drug and alcohol addiction. Because such kids are so high functioning, they become bored by traditional education methods and systems. They do remarkable things in their heads and yet that is their downfall, all too often. They become too clever for their own good. Given to bipolar disorder, they seek to self-medicate in order not to lose their high. The combination of high functioning and ADD or ADHD and dyslexia makes the risks of addiction exceptionally high.

Supporting Growth

Having these two persons in my life was and remains a life-changing and a life-challenging experience, especially in those years after the divorce from their mother. Now decades later we all seem to be at peace, though the differences between us are stark and often as challenging to both David and Deborah. In the early days, Kaye and I worked on many ways to live into our commitment to be co-parents. The kids and I had some issues to work out regarding my orientation and new life choices. Because they had lived among gay and lesbian folk in the parish, seeing two people of the same gender living together was not unusual to them. Deborah's definition of gay was "two people who love each other who are the same." Pretty complete. And because they had been around Buck for several years, it was not "unnatural" to see Daddy and Buck together.

It was only when they came to work with me one day at the U.S. Public Health Service office in Dallas, about two years after I had been working there, that they faced their first real experience of stigmatization and discrimination. Touring the facilities, several staffers invited them back to their stalls to learn about the work they did, "while Daddy was doing his job." During those moments, several staff members pressed the kids about how Daddy lived, and where and with whom. They responded openly, as kids do. I came upon this scene, much to the chagrin of those staffers. I went to my supervisor, an assistant surgeon general. He was outraged at such a violation and assured me that I was protected from harassment in the workplace. While the behavior of the other staff was deplorable, we both agreed that I really needed to debrief my children.

That evening, I had to explain to my kids what that questioning was about. They were sad. I implored them not to speak of my life and choices with others whom they had not met at my home. I was fearful of what such stigma or narrow-mindedness may do them. I wept that night, realizing that I had to tell a six-year-old and an eight-year-old about the harshness of other people's judgments. At the end of conversation, David's response was classic, "That's okay Daddy, we still love you no matter what anyone says." Deborah added, "Remember Dad, being gay is only about two people who are the same who love each other. What more can anyone say?"

Co-parenting with Kaye sort of worked until, two years after we separated and subsequently divorced, Kaye relocated to Houston, 300 miles away from Dallas, where we all had been living and, soon after, remarried. With my lack of further employment opportunities in Texas, being without a family locally and displaced professionally and socially, I was less inclined to remain in Dallas, so Buck and I moved to Washington, D.C., a year later, in 1992. But every Sunday evening at 7 p.m. I was on the phone, listening to the events of my children's lives from the preceding week and the anticipated events of the coming week. Their mother and lawyer and I had agreed to monthly payments for child support, fifty percent of my income, as well as two weeks of visitation in the summers and a few days after Christmas or Thanksgiving. I also showed up for special school or life events and accepted phone calls from either child as needed. Over the time that I was in South Africa, both David and Deborah came and stayed with me there. Throughout their twenties we traveled in various parts of the world every year to be with one another and to see the world together, until I returned from Europe in 2011.

Because of my understanding of what constituted a good and loving standard or an effective model of parenting as a child, I always felt myself to be at a distinct disadvantage. My mother's notion of parenting went something like this: "If you can survive this, you can survive anything." Kaye convinced me that parenting would go well for us, as our relationship at the beginning went very well as we struggled with authenticity and integrity, with purpose and compassion. Her core values reverted to family under any and all conditions, often loving others more than herself. I was similarly inclined but for different reasons. I never felt love in the confines of home.

Within three years, especially after David's birth, I was clearly at a loss as to how to make any proper or healthy responses to an over-active three-year-old daughter who had just gotten herself a new baby brother. A wise friend from my parish in Fort Worth commented while visiting us, "Ted, you are being too hard on her. She's trying hard to meet your expectations of being a good child, but you're laying a great deal on her, and ... she's just a little kid." I took it under advisement, but was not thoroughly convinced. Some months later, though, when Deborah was nearly four, I firmly chastised her for not calming down and for being a bit of a bother in her demands for attention. I sent her to her room for "time out" and there she remained for nearly an hour on her own recognizance. I could only hear her faintly mumbling something to herself. After a while she called out to me, "Daddy, I have something for you." And with that she brought out a piece of paper covered with smiley faces and flowers and a sun—carrying these words "im sarry DaDDy." It was her very first self-motivated piece of writing, and it was an apology to her father. I held it as the acidic tears of shame cascaded down my face and was reminded of my own tormented past and how this piece of artwork from my daughter summarized an important aspect of my own life experience, which seemed to be one long apology: "I'm sorry: sorry for being alive. I'm sorry for being here. I'm sorry for taking up space. I'm sorry for being a child…. I am so sorry."

From that moment on, I began to listen to my children differently, not wanting to replicate the reign of terror from my life called "growing up." I consciously moved myself to a place of deeper sensitivity, learning to perceive and understand a child's view of the world. Meanwhile I worked hard on being aware of play by encouraging it and even entering into it fully. Deborah seems to have gotten the core of my message as

Deborah Michelle (age 3), Easter 1985, just before David's birth.

she now practices the same with Selene. Attentive, loving, and laughing, she encourages and validates each moment of that baby girl's life. Just as laughter and giggling informed many of these activities, I recovered my own seemingly lost child through participation in the raising of my children. Yet I still held the line on discipline and responsibility. It often seemed a delicate but necessary balance: necessary for my own sanity, and delicate because of who was involved. On our trips and adventures together, like going to the movies, I gave each child an allowance so that they were free to make their own choices about treats and refreshments. Through their growing up I usually made inquiries about their infractions before meting out punishment. I quit raising my hand as a means of administering punishment; rather, I focused on isolation or separation from the main action as means for calming things and getting their attention. Every evening of our time together there would a quiet time for talking or learning about one another's lives, always followed by a story; first, me reading to them and then, over the years, them reading to me.

Real Parenting

Was it all that it could have been? No and yes. I could have remained in a marriage in which I found myself a captive to my own conscience and sense of duty, acting against my true nature of loving a man authentically as an "out" gay man. I could have tried to be a live-in dad, deeply frustrated with life. I could have fought the court's judgment of my acceptability as a parent. In those days judges "knew" that gay men were not acceptable fathers, or at least that's what the consensus understanding of the law in the State of Texas said. Perhaps I could have pushed harder for expanded rights and responsibilities as well as more frequent visiting privileges. But there was neither time nor money to battle a court in which my sexuality was being implicitly used against me.

I realized over time that the relationship between me and my children had the capacity to morph from being about the role of parent to a child to that of cultivating a friendship with two emerging young people. This transition began in their teens and continues to this day. I have never been a parent in the traditional sense perhaps, as they have their mom as well as her husband, who is a stepfather to them (although David has exploited that possibility more than Deborah). I have become a significant person in their lives by their choice and mine. I have little say in matters of power and authority. Rather, I have opted to become counselor and guide, sounding board, and one of their means to thinking things out in terms of relationship, change, and careers. I am perhaps a mentor when they wish to see me that way. Both offspring have come to see me as an experienced person with opinions and ideas, but one who is not necessarily insistent on getting my own way. This has been particularly painful for me in my dealing with my son through his struggles with addiction and alcoholism. I would do anything to have kept this horror from happening, but have been helpless to do so.

Darkness of Addiction

In those early years (ages 15–24) of David's addictions, I put up significant cash resources on several occasions for weeks or months in rehabilitation and detoxification programs. Thousands of dollars were expended in the name of recovery and hope. These various interventions worked as long as David was willing to live into the structured life of a halfway house. But the older he became, the less useful these approaches were. Now that he's in his thirties, with nearly two decades of addiction under his belt, these kinds of programs have been failures. Incarceration for extended periods in the legal system seems to have been as effective, at times. But, as David pointed out, "There are more drugs and alcohol available on the inside than on the outside." The greater and perhaps more costly challenge is summoning the emotional resources of facing into my own helplessness in the face of addiction and particularly the addiction of my own offspring. Addiction is the gift that keeps on taking, and taking, and taking for all who dare to stand within it with the addict. I know it would be easier to run away or turn one's back; many parents and siblings do. Living with addiction requires that all affected by it realistically admit their own helplessness and not capitulate to the psychic, spiritual, emotional, and physical blackmail of present and future scenarios the addicted person puts out there.

The challenge of addiction is that life is disordered and chaotic for everyone. One day David is up and the next he is down and armed with excuses aplenty. The fact remains that love is not a driving or saving influence here. David would like, at times, to believe that he is loving and supportive. Reciprocity, which many believe is crucial to most relationships in terms of giving and support, is not often the given between the addicted person and the family. Love, loyalty, honesty, and care are fleeting from the addicted one. Perhaps they are stillborn intentions for David because there is little or no follow-through on any aspect of relationship with his family. He seems to be developing it with the current person he cares for, having lost or alienated several other partners. Respect for anyone is rarely offered as he sincerely believes that many of us are stupid, naive or unworthy of it most of the time. Thus far, there has been no driving motivation for sobriety in David's life, save avoiding penal consequences, and even that assumption is now questionable.

Addiction to whatever the substance or behavior is constant and eternal. There will never be a day in his life when he will not be an addict or an alcoholic. The only choice he may be able to make is whether or not he chooses to act on his addiction in this moment, today. That is the heartbreaking reality of caring for an addict. We celebrate the good moments, with perhaps an unnecessary delight as there is always the hope that this will be the new way forward. Then we try to minimize the collapses and relapses and numerous returns to the madness created by the addiction. David has taught each of us that there is little that is eternal when it comes to the determination to stay sober and functioning, and that there is even less either hoped for or promised that is lasting.

It is not a matter of right and wrong for him, though always there is definitely the interplay of honesty and dishonesty. Rather, it is a matter of right here and right now versus tomorrow, the next days ahead, or even next week. Expediency over the immediate, today and right now over tomorrow are the operative time frames and places where decisions are made. Good intentions are always to be celebrated, but they may never come to pass. The longer they go unfulfilled, the less likely it is that these ambitions will ever become realities. Life is lived in the now, this moment, today. Whatever may transpire this afternoon or tonight has little to do with what is happening right now. What does it do to relationships, you may wonder? It makes shambles of them. Everything is true: nothing is true. Everything is predictable and nothing is. Alcoholics Anonymous, Narcotics Anonymous, and other self-help programs begin with the proposition that we need to give our lives over to a Higher Power (perhaps the God of our understanding) in order to find sanity. The family must do as much to find sanity as well.

Telling the Truth

Writing to David while he was in jail, I owned the challenges of parenting when I let him know:

It has been a painful journey to be sure and one which I have mishandled as much as any. I concede my unwillingness to let go of the notion of you as a smart, successful, and capable human being with endless opportunity. Recent events convince me that I am misguided in my optimism. I tend to overlook the facts of addiction and the reality of the disease of craving for drugs, alcohol, or something to change the reality of the moment. Clearly this truth overlooks the challenges of getting through a day in a creative and alive fashion without the use of stimulants, downers, or other mood-altering substances.

You diagnosed it rightly some months back by stating that you were genetically wired by my forebears and your mother's to be addicted. Your body and mind cannot tolerate these substances without creating insatiable cravings for them, as destructive as they are to your wellbeing. These are the ugly facts. I cannot apologize for your lack of will along these lines, only acknowledge that you are not in control and cannot make safe choices at this point…. By the same token, you actually cannot control my love for you. You can choose to dodge, deny, and discourage it, which you have tried to do repeatedly over these past several years; and you can lie until you don't know the truth from fiction, but you cannot convince me that loving you is a waste of my time and something for which you are not worthy.

On the contrary, from the day you were born, my choices about you were set. Namely, that I could and would love you, and learn the rest from you over time. You have taught me joy and delight in your achievements and in your self-reflection of your loves and sorrows. You have taught me that being faithful over the long haul is the only love that matters. You have taught me that acceptance is not always agreement and that agreement is not always permission. You have taught me how to reach through the denial and stimulate the telling of truth. All I seek for you or from you is for you to find your own happiness—as elusive as it may be—and be prepared to follow it. All I hope for you is to find your self and learn to trust that self to a place of fulfillment and peace.

Over time, I have had to learn repeatedly that loving is not merely a matter of reciprocity. Love must be freely given without expectation of fulfillment or return. Loving a child has called me out of my self and my own painful past of being a child to becoming an embodied adult. Wrongly holding a model of recovery and professional expectation for David that he may or may not choose to reach or may not be able to reach has become a dangerous and cruel form of loving. He will have to set his own goal for wellness and achieve it whatever way works for him. I cannot let my love be contingent on what he does or how he does it. To do otherwise is essentially selfish and remarkably lacking in grace and acceptance. It has taken more than seventeen years of struggling with him to realize this fact, own up to it, and seek his forgiveness for my assumptions and expectations.

Since his release from jail three years ago we continued to engage and retreat in renegotiating our way of being with one another. In the past year, silence has ensued. The law initially limited his ability to travel out of state in order that he not miss any of his probation office appointments. While it was wonderful to see him sober for a while, it was terrible because of my anticipation of a fall, which came days after he returned to Texas. He remained sober for a time, but has again fallen under the influence and is awaiting the determination of his fate by the law courts. But what he will do in his life and how he will do it as an adult will take us both down roads we have not traveled before, but not before we struggle a bit more with life as it really is for him.

David Warren and Selene cuddling together in Galveston, Christmas, 2017.

It is difficult to resist comparing these two, for they are a study in contrasts. David's sister Deborah Michelle is an inveterate planner. She identifies moves and necessities way down the road. On the other hand, she married Jeremy after spending many years together. I was 34 when Deborah was born, so her timing is pretty consistent with mine. It seems that it took each of us time to decide that life was OK and safe to proceed with child-bearing/raising. Such a commitment says there is faith in the future and in the relationship. As a result of my divorce from her mother, I can readily understand Deborah's previous reticence about family and relationship and mothering. She and Jeremy have been together for thirteen years and then married in the weeks before Selene's birth. It is evident that they were ready for family. Her mother and I had been together for thirteen years before we separated. I believe the coincidence is intentional at some deeply felt level. I was initially reluctant to officiate at the ceremony. But Deborah insisted, saying, "Dad, we wanted you because you know exactly what we need and how it should look." I tried to. More importantly, though, they agreed to undergo referral for counseling before the wedding to ensure that they started out on level ground. I am delighted and confident for them and hopeful for their future together.

Dark Night and Restoration

Deborah, more highly strung than David in her response to things, is usually instantaneous, often taking too much to heart and believing that she is truly unworthy. While incredibly competent at many things, she has always judged herself rather harshly on what she could master. She and David share some common DNA on this harshness of self-judgment, though she beats him on levels of self-recrimination. Perhaps the hardest time of her life, as it is for most people, was adolescence. Responses to any challenge to her authority were dramatic, decisive, and often over the top. Stomping up and down stairs or through the house, perfected since childhood, was a great technique by which anger could be expressed. Door slamming was added in adolescence for effect. But again, that is adolescence.

I learned the hard way though that real outrage and shame was often expressed in silence and non-disclosure. At no time was it more unbearable than when she tried to overdose on a handful of Tylenol tablets taken as the result of sexual assault by a classmate from school. Standing in the kitchen, near her mother, talking about school and life, she quietly and without alerting her mom, downed such a significant amount of medication that 12 hours later the physicians at Children's Hospital in Houston informed her mother that her liver and kidneys were so severely damaged and that in all likelihood she would become completely comatose and die within 24 hours.

Deb had become violently ill about eight hours after taking the medications. When Kaye called me in Washington, I sprang into action and hastily arranged for a flight to Houston four hours later. Shocked and horrified, my friends and staff in D.C. contacted the presiding bishop, Edmond Browning, to inform him of this unfolding tragedy in Houston.

He immediately deployed the local bishop in Houston, who then called upon a number of his local clergy, to visit and be with the family until my arrival later that day. While that was comforting in some respects, it was terribly upsetting to hear from Kaye about my colleagues offering constant prayers and unfounded assurances, comfort and support with promises of God's power over a child, whom medicine had deemed near death, without any prospect for hope.

In that terrible moment of impending tragedy, I found a deeper faith than I had ever known when—after absorbing the facts of Deborah's hopeless condition, and listening carefully to her mother and brother about what happened without any of us knowing the "why" of it until years later—I realized that I would lose my daughter by her own hand. She was in and out of a coma on my arrival and had only aroused briefly, retreating back into her death-like sleep. Because she had done this horrific thing to herself, the doctors informed us that she would not be eligible for a transplant to save either the liver or kidneys.

As the night wore on the impact of what we were facing was becoming evident. I insisted that Kaye and David and Buck go to a hotel nearby to rest. I assured them all that I would call when the situation became more serious. Kaye was absolutely exhausted, having been alone with Deb since she became violently ill in the early morning hours, and had been handling everything ever since admission to the hospital. She resisted leaving, then gratefully accepted the time away to rest. Throughout the remainder of the night I sat next to the bed in the ICU and waited. The doctors expected Deborah to begin slipping away by around five or six the next morning, given her poor kidney and liver results. Her body was shutting down.

Helpless, I called on the God of my understanding, first apologizing that insistent prayers could change the natural course of anyone's life, particularly that of my dying daughter. I could not accept a god who was nothing more than a celestial bellboy awaiting our direction or request. Sobbing quietly at the impending tragedy of my daughter's death, I found myself sending up a keening prayer that I would be given the strength to let her go when the time came; and then, to be enabled to commend her life to God's permanent care and keeping. Empty handed, bereft, I then asked to learn trust and acceptance for the encroaching horror. There was nothing more for which to pray in that desperate moment. It must have been around midnight, as the hospital was still and movement minimal. I then fell asleep holding her hand.

Around 3 a.m., I was awakened by a sudden stir of movement in Deborah's bed. She was marginally alert in that dreamlike space of a pre-dawn awakening. She quietly asked, "Daddy, what are you doing here? And, where is here?" I explained that she was in an intensive care unit and that this was Children's Hospital in Houston. I went on to tell her that she had become seriously ill after taking too many Tylenol tablets. And that her mom brought her in an ambulance to the hospital.

"Oh, yes," she said, "I remember. I felt terrible about myself and everything. I decided that I shouldn't be here anymore." And with that, she became drowsy again and started drifting off. Were these to be her last words? Then she said, "I'm really glad to see you, Daddy. By the way, remember how you would put your hand on the places where I hurt myself when I was little?" I nodded yes. "Would you put your hand on this place [she indicated that it was just below the ribcage] where everything hurts a lot and on my lower back?" This was exactly where the liver and kidneys are located. So I put my hands where she instructed while she lay on her side, and then felt the heat move from my hands to her cold, clammy body. With that she smiled at me and fell asleep.... Back into that dreamless death-like sleep.

I sat there rather dumbfounded realizing that this might be the last time I would ever speak to her. I never said, "I love you" or "goodbye." Filled with self-recrimination, I tried to rouse her to say that much, but she slept through it.

Around 5 a.m., one of the medical technicians came in to draw blood, followed by the night nurses who, one after another, checked her vitals, saying nothing. At 6 a.m., the same team returned with more tests and thorough checking. Deborah was breathing normally and felt slightly warmer in her bed. But she was still asleep. Kaye arrived around 7 a.m. and again, there was another round of tests and checking vitals.

At 7:45 a.m., the physicians and nurses of her team arrived *en masse* and Deborah awoke, but this time it was as if she had a perfect night's sleep. One of the number then spoke. "We don't know what to say to you. Yesterday, we told you that things today would be radically different from the way they are at this moment. We don't know why. Yesterday our tests showed that there was no liver or kidney function. Today the results are absolutely normal. We've checked and re-checked and everything is normal. Kidneys and livers damaged the way hers were just don't rejuvenate and recover. Hers did. We would like to move her to a semi-private room that is unoccupied for continued observation for today. She can go home tomorrow."

Kaye looked at me and I at her. We both cried tears of thanksgiving. Deborah was mystified about why we were so tearfully delighted. The "how" and "why" of what happened have remained a medical mystery. Through her pregnancy and then delivery of Selene and before there have been no recurrences of her health issues. Everything was normal. Years later though, she would tell us of her assault and the shame and fearsomeness of it, though she had no real memory of the hospital experience. Some therapy visits helped her come to terms with the fact that she had tried to do something horrible, which could have ended her life and that this effort had failed. The underlying cause, resulting from the assault, would only be revealed years after she was in secure relationship with the man who would one day become her husband.

I would like to think I know what actually happened that night, but I have refused to say until now. Somehow it didn't seem to be my place to say anything about those events until now. As a remarkable postscript though, in October 2017, Deborah "came out"—being a regional manager with her company—in the #metoo movement. I am grateful that she has healed to such a place that she can self-identify as both victim and victor.

Curiously, one of my delights in Deborah since early in her life is that she taught me the real meaning of human egocentricity. Namely, from her earliest days she acted in the sincere belief that I was born about ten minutes later than she. Thus, she has had to show me how I was to be the beneficiary/learner and that she was the teacher. However, during her pregnancy there was an opportunity for me to speak and offer insight and direction when I was allowed to share my experience of parenting with her for the first time. Throughout that remarkable season, I wrote to Deborah weekly, describing my experience of parenting and my thoughts about child rearing, pregnancy, and relationship. The day Selene was born, I wrote a letter, welcoming her to the family:

> You have been born into the charmed circle of a family of love and deep commitment to you and your life. You will never be alone and never be without love. From conception to birth and from this day forward, you have been ensconced and embraced from your conception in love. Even when you feel most alone and very vulnerable, love is overshadowing and enveloping you in wonder, miracle, and grace. If you are ever fearful, call out and we all will be there for you, particularly your mom and dad, who are busy tonight just cooing with your birth in this sacred moment.

Deborah is quite a good mom, judging from her conversations with me and her mother about mothering and parenting and through my observing her during infrequent visits to her home. We were bonded in new ways through the pregnancy; it seems that I finally got the recognition that I might have had, if I had been around. Five months after she was born, Selene was baptized by me in Galveston, thrilling me that her parents saw the importance of a good spiritual foundation for her life as much as a good home to help her establish herself in the world. This is a sign of growth for all of us.

Respecting Differences

It is evident to me that neither of my offspring is going to do things that necessarily fulfill the expectations of their parents. Deborah has worked incredibly hard to make her life what she wants it to be. She has set both long-term and near-term goals. She and Jeremy have established a home base from which they operate their lives, and they have made room for the bumps of unexpected situations and outcomes. They have faced loss together with thoughtful and heartfelt grief and have welcomed the wonders of life with full embrace. As Deborah grows her own greater autonomy as a woman, a wife, a mother, a daughter, she has found a way to exert her own integrity and purposefulness without necessarily blaming any of us for questionable outcomes. I would like to believe that she has been motivated by the work her parents have devoted to achieving some satisfaction with their own lives with unabashed honesty and purposefulness.

This is all so different than what I had expected. As I mentioned earlier in this book, I once had what is called a "root dream"—one that established the lines and standards of a new norm and from that point reshaped the life that followed. This dream happened on the eve of my own coming out as a gay man. In that dream I believed that I had died and was facing judgment, or at least what I thought judgment to be. The space was filled with light, and out of the light or brightness I was asked, "Do you have any regrets?" I was shown my whole life as if it were a movie until the moment of my death. Then I was asked again, "Do you have any regrets?" I said, "Yes. I really want to know how the story comes out for my children." So the film was forwarded through their lives as children, adolescents, and young adults and as parents. I was asked again, "Do you have any regrets?" Once again, I said, "Yes. I really need to know how their story comes out." Once again, the film was forwarded to them being middle aged, as I was when the dream took place. Again, the voice asked: "Are there any regrets?" I was about to answer "Yes" again, but instead started laughing at my folly, realizing that I would always have regrets about not seeing what happens to the grandchildren and great-grandchildren and their children's children. In that moment, I knew that I would no longer live my life for what I didn't know and couldn't see. Rather, I would live for each moment and savor it. Thus far I have had no regrets.

Letting Go: The Secret of Self-Control

Letting go of supposed control and expectations is another aspect of parenting that receives little note. Attempts at control had to be let go quickly because my children often threw off the yoke of my need to control them, or my miserable attempts at it, long before I was ready to give it up. On one of my WHO trips, I routed myself through Houston so that I could see them, now in their twenties. Deborah and Jeremy had been together nearly five years at this point. I had arranged for David to meet me at the airport.

After a warm greeting and finally on our way to meet up with his sister for dinner, he said, "Dad, you've got to acknowledge who Jeremy is in Deborah's life and that he is here to stay."

I muttered something inane in defense of my poor behavior, but

David would not let it go. He said again, "You've got to stop calling him 'what's his name' as it is really getting to Deborah."

"Why?"

"Because he loves her and she loves him. You may not have noticed this, but it is to your benefit."

"Why?" I intoned again.

"Because your daughter, my sister, is really high maintenance, and he likes doing it because he loves her."

Deborah Michelle, Jeremy Lee and Selene Ember Rose Roberts. Thanksgiving in Tyler, Texas, 2018.

Stunned by the insightfulness and candor of a brother about his sister, I assented. From that day forward I referred to him by his name—Jeremy—and actually began to take an interest in him, all this after five years. Today, I am grateful to say that I love him and I love them together. Over the past decade, Jeremy and I have become close and caring with one another. He has indicated that he enjoys our private conversations and I confess I was delighted when he told me to call him "son" after he and Deborah were married. He is a thoughtful professional, being an investigating officer for child protective services. He sees and has to intervene in some horrific family situations to protect children. It is a grueling and thankless job, but he does it with grace and thoughtfulness. He adores Deborah and dotes constantly on his daughter. But most of all, he is a rock: solid, consistent, purposeful and strong. I am grateful that he is in my life, too.

I said that it is still hard for me to let go of trying to make life right for my offspring and their family of significance, and that I often try to shape them to a particular vision or expectation not of their own making, because it is hard to let go. Wonderfully, there are boundaries all around, and each of my children will remind me of them when I have overstepped them. They are not shy in calling me out.

There is no secret to parenting as I have come to know it. The fact is that each one who tries will inevitably get it wrong at some point or another. The only way to stay in the game of family is to accept the fact that one will lose what they may believe in the moment to be utterly important. Over time, the notion of what was important changes. It is important, though, to remain loving, even when the children are ugly and most unpleasant to be around—as in adolescence. Growth for all of us comes only when we let that love become transformed. These remarkable people—David and Deborah—are not necessarily representative of our own highest intentions and personal goals; rather, they are unique creatures, tempered perhaps by their genetic inheritance and the nurture of being Kaye's and my offspring. By the ways of the world, while we may have the opportunity to raise them for a period of time, the reality is that they will have made many of their own choices without consultation and will even make choices that either parent would not have made. The goal of child-rearing or child-raising should to be to bring them up in such ways that they think on their own, are confident in their choices, are willing to accept the consequences, and through it all in some way choose to be decent human beings. It's a lot to take on and even more to say grace over, but the journey is finally about opening one's own heart to trust and hope in the future—mine and theirs!

I doubt that I could have achieved very much of lasting value in this life had I not learned to be a father to my children. In its day that concept would run counter to norm as gay men were often thought of as self-centered, self-absorbed, and not capable of child-raising because of their obsessions with their own sexuality. At least that's how the courts and divorce lawyers often cast it. I am grateful that this is not so much the case today, as there are an increasing number of transgender, gay, and lesbian parents across America who are enviable role models of good parenting, Even now I look at my son and daughter with the same understanding that many parents have of sorrow and regret, deep admiration and gratitude, and delight for their willingness to educate me in the ways of being their father.

Learnings and Faith

The lessons of the parenting experience are relatively simple. Good parenting has not changed in that it requires a willingness to make life better than it was in the past. Parenting requires the investment and trust in tomorrow and a deep desire to improve the world, the community, and the family. Constancy demands staying in the process, even when the cost of staying in seems high. Being an adult and taking on the role of parent requires an indomitable spirit, a willingness to openly admit wrong or failure, and a strange adventuresome delight in starting over, again and again. Being a parent is an act of faith: faith in God, faith in tomorrow, faith in one's self, and faith in the offspring, no matter how much they test it. David and Deborah have afforded me that rare opportunity to learn from them and with them. This learning has been crucial to the perfecting grace that has happened to my life. Without them, I would have been lost and more fearful than I usually am. Without them, I would not have had to re-prioritize my life as often as I have. Without them, I would have been half a man, half a human, and half a priest. They taught me grace in the face of utter contradiction and frustration, and they taught me that love is forever and unconditional. Sometimes I actually live into these truths and celebrate what is there. In a recent encounter with David, he stated rather forthrightly, "You know, Dad, we trust that you will always be there." And to date, by the grace of God and extending myself through a broken heart, I have tried to be present.

X

Prayer and Faithfulness

If your soul is awakened, then you realize that this is the house of your real belonging. Your longing is safe there. Belonging is related to longing. If you hyphenate belonging, it yields a lovely axiom for spiritual growth; Be-Your-Longing. Longing is a precious instinct in the soul. Where you belong should always be worthy of your dignity. You should belong first in your own interiority.
—John O'Donohue, *Anam Ċara: A Book of Celtic Wisdom*

What can you say when two souls meet on the way to paradise? While being seated on our early Sunday morning British Airways flight to Jo'burg (Johannesburg) in 2002, we recognized each other by our apparel. He was the very well-known Rebbe Mendel Lipskar, the chief Hasidic Rebbe (Chabad Lubavitch) of South Africa, replete with his large round velvet hat and long grey-and-white beard over his long-tailed black *bekishe* kaftan coat and the tassels of his *tzitzit*, a traditional undergarment, showing at the waist. Me? Also dressed all in black—suit, shirt, shoes, and socks—and of course, the telltale symbol of the solid white clerical collar accompanied by a cross on a chain over my chest. I was to preach that morning in South Africa's largest, most famous township, Soweto.

Prayer and Tradition

Within moments of take-off he put his *tallit* (a fringed prayer shawl) over his shoulders and then began to *daven* (Yiddish *doven* or *daven*—to recite the Jewish prayers while bending or swaying forward

and back). Meanwhile I opened my Prayer Book and began mouthing
the Morning Office, occasionally *davening* to the rhythm of the prayers.
He looked over at me and I at him, acknowledging our mutual expressions of devotion, and then we went on with our prayers. This was a
rare moment of pure recognition and respect for our various callings
and traditions. In that moment we found ourselves caught up, gazing
into the pale light just before sunrise. After our time in prayer and med-
itation was completed, followed by a moment of contemplation, he asked
me about my *daven*. I explained that my grandfather was a Jew who had
married a gentile. Neither practiced their religions with their offspring;
however, after I turned two and until his death when I was five, he would
come to take me away early on Saturday mornings. Years later I discovered, literally by accident, that he had begun the morning by taking me
to *schul* (synagogue, house of Jewish worship), where I would be seated
on his lap. He would quietly recite the prayers in my ear, *davening* as he
prayed.

The rebbe said, "You know, he gave you his faith in that act of praying. Even though no one would acknowledge him as part of the *minyan*
[official gathering to make a morning prayer] because he was considered
'dead' by the community, he was still able to transmit his faith." I sadly
nodded, acknowledging his understanding.

I then continued, "I had figured this out long after his death, when
I attended my first synagogue service as an adult. It was during the High
Holy Days—Yom Kippur—in Brooklyn. I was a special guest of the rabbi,
whom I knew in the neighborhood where I was working. I found myself
davening during the opening portion of the prayers." I then told him
about the broken family with more passion than I knew I had about this
"family secret."

"Such a gift you have been given and yet ... with such pain and loss
and such estrangement," he replied with sadness in his voice.

We continued to speak of this and of other holy things. We told
each other some of the secrets of our souls in our animated "small talk."
After some time of conversation, he admitted to me, "Rarely have I
encountered a follower of Jeshua [Jesus] who so recognized the place
of the faith of Abraham and his own place in the world and that of others.... With such respect, trust, and openness."

At some point in our mutual sharing I visibly withdrew into myself, pausing with a question on the tip of my tongue but failing to articulate it. "It is obvious something is troubling you," he said. "What is it?"

I blurted out that I had a long-unspoken question about prayer (*tefillah*, meaning something more akin to self-examination and self-disclosure to God than the written or formal prayer often prayed by Anglicans). Calling my hesitancy into question, he insisted that I ask. "Okay then; while we have said our prayers this morning, I would like to know how to really pray; that is, how to bring one's self, one's whole being, into proximity with Y-W-H [God]."

The Three Questions

After some moments of reflection he responded slowly and deliberately, as if conveying a great secret. "I have three questions for you." I nodded as it is legendary that rebbes always seem to have three questions. "So," he continued, "do you have a teacher for prayer? Do you have a friend with whom you pray? And do you have a student to whom you teach prayer?"

At that moment, what had not been working for me in South Africa, or anywhere else for that matter, became as clear as the dawning day. I said "No" to all three questions.

"Well, then," he went on, "No wonder you have deep questions about true prayer. Here you are, a man who represents Y-W-H in every aspect of life and who talks about life and living in passionate terms, and probably also talks to Y-W-H all the time, but is terribly isolated and removed from the love of others. Here you are, a man who is having difficulty feeling the efficacy of that prayer. Is it any wonder? To pray, Ted, you must be grounded in all three of these definitive and distinctive relationships. You need them, for these are the means by which we maintain balance. These means are the way to keep you anchored in this world where you must live!"

A deep reverential silence fell over us as I again turned my head to gaze out the cabin window to the dawning landscape of the South African frontier, tears silently running down my face. In the two years of working in southern Africa I found myself profoundly alone and felt separated from all that I knew and understood. I was not fluent or even cognizant in any of the eleven official languages of South Africa. Even my English was American and not the proper English of the British and their heirs. Yet, in the dark nights, in spite of being alone—now more than two years from having had a partner at home—I found myself drifting aimlessly into what appeared to be a deepening, almost mystical relationship with what I understood to be God. But I couldn't be sure. Gone were the pious acts and practiced formalisms of written prayer. The relational nature of this intimate experience of conversation through consciousness of the presence of holiness had become manifest in my almost self-less and spontaneous acts of praying and devotion at any time around the clock. I was acutely aware that I was no longer alone and yet I felt, at the same time, the deep and fearful sense of an unfathomable distance between my self and the holy. Having come from years of struggle and estrangement, desire and disappointment, zeal and abandonment with my own faith tradition and my faith in God, while adhering to the practices of the Book of Common Prayer steadfastly and routinely, I was still starving for validation of this deeper sense of the connection. While I admit that it was happening in what felt to be a natural and almost organic way, it was not in any way what I had sought or come to expect. I had not prepared for anything like this to happen for all the decades of prayer in which I engaged. So I doubted it.

Memories, Dreams and Visions of God

So how did I get to this question? How did I have the audacity to put something so personal and core to my being before a rebbe on a flight early on a Sunday morning? My earliest memory of being about the work of knowing or experiencing God or the immanent/transcendent, or in today's parlance, non-locality, began when I was a very small child. I suspect I was somewhere between the ages of two and four. I still cannot recall whether it was a dream or a fact as it had the quality of both and it still does! But I have corroborated through my mother that, from early childhood through near adolescence, I was a very active sleep talker and sleepwalker from my earliest time of walking, around nine months old. The memory of this encounter has lived with me in such detail and clarity over my entire lifetime from these earliest recollections. It goes like this:

I was in bed seated, but bowed down to the forehead in front of the sitting figure of the Buddha. He was seated on a lotus before me. He was communicating with me in feelings and thoughts and intuitions, but not with audible words per se. I recall feeling peaceful and trusting and, after some time of devotion, gently crept into his lap and lay down, secure under his upwardly cupped hands. I can still feel the warmth of that fulfilled and safe feeling, secure in the knowledge that I am eternally loved by the universe in all of its manifestations. I was and am secure in faith and love. Over the years since, I have had visions of Kali, the Virgin Mary, Ganesh, Moses, Elijah, and Jesus, all while being in prayerful waking or dream-

Receiving the blessing of Swami Agnivesh at the Decent Care seminar at Vevey, Switzerland, 2006.

ing states. That I am loved and welcomed into the sacred fellowship of saints and angels, seers and prophets, martyrs and heroes has been and still remains the heart of this core teaching, without question.

The violence of family and experiences of life in the world have been considerable contradictions to my inner sense of belonging and wholeness. But I learned early that the world—particularly occupied by adults as it is—does not always tell the truth. The most formidable religious figure in my upbringing was my mother's "fresh off the boat from Ireland" Aunt Marge, otherwise known as Sister Berenice, a Sister of Charity. She was the sister of my mother's mother, Josephine Reilly, who had died in 1932 of cholera in New York City. As youngsters, my brothers and I were regularly called upon by our mother to go see the old aunty (who, as I now think of it, was younger than I am today; perhaps, to me then, she simply had no any age at all). She had always resided in convents attached to schools and hospitals, as the members of her order were teachers and nurses. She was a mysterious lady, covered in black veils and a voluminous, formless black gown, with a cincture (belt) that had a very large rosary with a large crucifix at the end, displaying a rather vivid Jesus on the cross. It was forbidding and somewhat terrifying.

But it was clear that she was a person of power: great, mysterious, dark power. So it was no surprise when she asked us during one of our visits, "Do you want to see Jesus?" I had always suspected that she had a secret, and I wanted to know it. Her invitation was over the top, and I responded with a loud affirmative "Yes!"

My brothers were less enthusiastic, still distrusting this dark force of nature or God. My mother just stared blankly and quietly assented to her aunty's request. As a member of this convent, Aunt Marge had been chosen to be the sacristan of the chapel. It meant that she also had

Aunt Marge (Sister Berenice) holding Ted, December 30, 1948.

a string of keys, one of which ensured safe passage into the nuns' chapel. There on a high altar was a large shining brass tabernacle (a cylindrical box, bejeweled, with a locked door containing sacramental bread and wine already consecrated at mass). We were quietly escorted to the outer rail of the altar and told that we could not enter into the altar space, as it was a "holy place."

Obediently and expectantly we stood gazing heavenward as she asked again, "Do you want to see Jesus?" I yelled out, almost in a swoon, "Yes!" She inserted a large key into the tabernacle and turned it, opening the door, revealing a small curtain blocking the view of what or who was actually in there. She extended her hand, reaching through the curtain. "Do you want to see Jesus?" Now anticipating what I assumed to be a Tom Thumb–sized creature, I nodded eagerly and whispered, "Yes … oh yes…. Yes!" She reached in further and fumbled with something. Then she suddenly withdrew her hand, slammed the door, turned the key and said, "You can't see Jesus! You are not a Catholic!"

Dumbstruck and shocked at this sudden turn, we ran from the chapel to our waiting mother. Crying and moaning loudly, I said, "I can't see Jesus, I'm not a Catholic." I insisted, "I want to be Catholic," having no idea of what one was or what it meant. My mother looked at her aunt; the nun shook her head in rage. With that we promptly left the convent without so much as another word. All the way home in the car, I cried for my loss of Jesus while my mother muttered to herself. Upon our arrival at home she addressed us in the back seat, "You will never speak of this again, especially to your father. You will never be Catholics, or anything else for that matter, as long as I have something to say about it." Then she muttered again, "Damn Catholics, they respect nothing and no one."

Years later, I was in theological school and in my early twenties. That same aunt lay dying as a bed-bound invalid. For some reason I felt compelled to go see her in her last days. Pleased to see me, now dressed all in black myself, she moaned, "Oh, what a loss for all of us and for God. You could have been a Catholic and not one of those heretic priests from the Church of England. Only then would you know God. As it is, you are a heretic!"

I looked at her, more tenderly now, having mastered the mysteries of the sacramental celebration and ritual acts of the Lord's Supper (the Eucharist, the Mass) and replied, "But Aunty, I am a priest—albeit a Protestant by your standards—and I am the only one from your family or from any church for that matter who is here for you right now."

She closed her eyes, "I suppose so," she muttered. "But 'tis a pity anyway." We never saw one another in this life again.

Beyond Religious Institutions

That experience helped me understand the mystery of adults and denominations, of traditions, biases, and prejudices, and clearly opened my eyes to many things. But then I was called out to move beyond the institution and my institutional safeguards. Only weeks after the catastrophe of being fired from my position as canon missioner for AIDS in South Africa, I found myself walking the Camino de Santiago in Spain.

Santiago de Compostela is a city in the far west of Spain in the region called Galicia, where it is alleged in tradition and history that the brother of Jesus came to evangelize the locals on this outermost edge of the Roman Empire. In 1100 AD, Bishop Theodore had a vision that this place is where the bones of St. James (Sant Iago) were returned. His reputed remains now lie interred in the crypt of what is, today, the cathedral. Ever since Theodore's declaring the cathedral's crypt containing the bones a place of holiness and remembrance, the site has been one of pilgrimage and devotion. For more than a thousand years, pilgrims have made their way to pray there as an act of devotion, penance, absolution, intercession, and mystical prayer. Some have walked the pilgrim's journey of over 800 kilometers (500 miles) as an act of contrition or as an act of nothing more than pure physical exercise and endurance. Regardless, after walking for 20 to 40 days from St. Jean Pied de Port on the French-Spanish border, one believes whatever is necessary about the journey to Santiago. It's long and grueling and takes everything one has and usually a great deal more.

But that has been said often. I was still reeling from the impact of the losses in South Africa and smarting from the rejection and subsequent eviction. I decided that I would not disclose myself as a priest on this sojourn. Rather, I was just a pilgrim in search of … something. One of the things pilgrims learn early on in walking El Camino is that no two people walk this journey in the same way at the same pace. In some cases, this difference can make forward-going quite frustrating for walking partners, couples in love, and even married persons. I saw it all on the road.

My planned walking partner was Kent Smith, my landlord in South Africa, who had initially suggested that I might want to make this walk as a way of making peace with my South African experience. Kent was very fit and walked with his longish legs on a 6-foot, 3-inch frame and a feverish energy to "conquer the road." He was now celebrating his 50th year of life, and it was evident that I could not keep up with him and his blistering pace. So we lost each other the day after celebrating my

55th birthday, on a section of the Roman road outside Estella (some five days out). We reconnected 26 days later in Santiago!

All at once I was alone and lost, having simply followed an unpaved road out into the countryside. When I realized the mistake (an hour or two into the diversion), I turned back but then chose to take what appeared to be a shortcut through a farmer's field and over newly plowed furrows (as much as two feet deep) to the several-storied white cross commemorating the martyrs of the Spanish Revolution, high on the mountaintop ahead. What separated me was a field of thorns and brambles. Looking up, I prayed for help on the road for the first time: "Give me a way forward." Then suddenly there came a convocation of eagles soaring and diving in flight, no doubt for the carrion in the plowed field behind me. However, they dropped and dodged in a pattern which suggested to me that I follow them. For more than an hour I climbed uphill unscathed, through the brambles and thorns, to the cross at the very top. Upon my arrival, the eagles circled a few times and vanished, leaving me a wide-open view of where I had gotten lost, where I came from, and the way I needed to go. From that moment on, I came to understand that assessing my reality and asking for help was not an altogether inappropriate means of asking for something akin to divine guidance. And each real prayer of this nature was answered on the road over the next month.

By day 20, entering the province of Galicia, I was spent. All complaints and excuses—about everything that hadn't worked for me out there—seemed to dissipate with the morning fog. Praying as I did daily early in the morning, I plaintively called out to the heavens, "Is there no one out here who speaks English?" Indeed, after weeks of barely managing, communicating in faltering Spanish, French and German, I wanted to relax a bit and just hear English spoken. Up ahead, on the upward side of the summit leading to a vast descent into the tidal lowlands of the province, I heard English being spoken for the first time. Quickening my pace, I caught up to a man and woman arguing. I asked, "American?" "No, Irish," he said. I looked at her. "American?" "No, Mexican," she answered quickly. We walked a while. Rob "Kyran the Artist" Morgan of Galway Bay and Evelyne Rodriguez y Ortega of Mexico City began a conversation that lasted 12 days, until the conclusion of their Camino journey, and it continues to this day, 16 years later. I learned that he was the much-discussed runner on the Camino—he left his cell-phone in one town, journeyed to the next town 15 miles away, and after realizing it was gone he raced back to retrieve it, and then he returned, all in the same day. Evelyne, the former treasurer of Mexico, was walking to gain perspective of the world and her service to it and think through, literally, the next steps in her life. This was similar to my reason for walking. Rob was also looking at a different future as a mathematician and psychologist. All three of us were searching for a new way to be in the world and let go of our pasts for the grief and delight they contained. For the next fortnight we were close, walking daily, and dining together every evening, revealing the most intimate aspects of our lives. Laughter and tears were always a feature of the day just past. Rob and Evelyne were always way out front walking, but I usually caught up by the midday meal. And so it went until we entered the city of Santiago, singing the lyrics, *Dona Nobis Pacem* (Grant Us Peace), the last words of the *Agnus Dei* (Lamb of God), sung at Mass before receiving Holy Communion.

Perhaps the hardest challenge of those sun-filled days on the Camino became a serious contradiction to my faith and spirituality. It was my complete loss of memory of the most basic Christian prayers and psalms, canticles and passages, which I had committed to memory over more than three and a half decades of priesthood and ministry. Some of us clergy actually pride ourselves on our memory of specific passages or prayers from our written traditions. I was, for all intents and purposes, struck dumb by the mere walking of a road. The only words which came to me happened spontaneously and almost miraculously daily at noon with the ringing of the bells, as they do across Spain and Portugal, for the *Angelus*. Being struck dumb, as one who is so verbal is in itself a rather fantastic notion, much less an actual experience. But for 33 days, I could not remember any of the liturgical language I had recited by rote for decades. Somehow, it was the finishing touch of what I needed to be an anonymous pilgrim (in Spanish, *peregrino*) on the Camino. At 12 noon each day, I absented myself from fellow walkers and said the *Angelus*.

When I attempted to pray at any other time it was conversational and usually a complaint or challenge, like, "Why are we doing this?" To which the universe often responded with a gentle but firm, insistent internal voice saying, "Keep walking." The anonymity also allowed me

End of the road. Evelyne Rodriguez y Ortega of Mexico City and Ted Karpf finishing the Camino walk (800 km) to Santiago after 32 days of walking, October 2003.

to listen and observe a bit more closely than I might have otherwise done. And for a week it worked. With Kent gone I was, in every respect, on my own. I met up with folk, walked with them a while, and then moved on. About eight days later, in the midafternoon, I entered a small village on the outskirts of the city of Burgos, home to El Cid and St. Teresa of Avila. I asked for water from the *hospitalero* (the person who is the guest master of an *albuerge* or *refugio,* refuge or guest house); her name, Sybille Yates, from Germany. She is still on the Camino as the lay coordinator of the Anglican Chaplaincy for spiritual services support of pilgrims sojourning to Santiago. She replied in her thick German accent, "That is the worst Spanish I have ever heard. Where are you from?"

I quickly responded, "From South Africa most recently and actually from the United States."

She then said, "Well, Ted, we've been waiting for you for several days. You are to say Mass here this evening." Somewhat flummoxed by the greeting, she went on to explain that Kent had been there several days before and announced that I would be coming along soon. Thus my coming or showing up somewhere had been foretold, literally! But I really thought I was a stranger out there and thought that I had rather liked being invisible in the world.

Over the next two days in that refuge, my blisters were dressed and began to heal. But more importantly I found my voice after days and days of self-imposed silence. That first night I preached about Jesus also being on the road, as I asked the assembled 50 or so pilgrims, "Who is Jesus for you today on this road?" A question that would haunt me from that day to this. I didn't think I was asking a universal, once-for-all-time question. But I was. I was outed as a priest from that night, and my vocation would recur as a driving theme from that evening forward.

A widely held experience of walking the Camino is that you will meet everyone you will see on the entire journey within the first week. Some days you are two or three ahead, and on others two or three behind. In a curious way, it forced me to get in touch with the fact that I had actually been shattered by my summary eviction from South Africa, and to my mind the Church as co-conspirator was doing what the Church does: abusing its people and me, in particular, ending my work before I was finished. Nonetheless, meeting Jesus in the faces and hearts of my fellow pilgrims and sojourners gave me glimpses of life, of connections heretofore not imagined. On the road, I found my baptism becoming my work of the world. This fundamental truth is what had brought me to ministry in the first place, 30 years before.

Why Are You Here?

It was no accident that I was on the road. Indeed, it is an apt metaphor for the journey on which we all are sojourners and which is lived out every day of our lives, whether we are aware of it or not. "Why are you out here?" asked Pascal, a young pilgrim, one day as we ambled along the road to Pamplona early on. I had been out walking for only two days. I told him the story of how I got there, even though my feet already hurt, my back ached from the too-heavy backpack, and I had blisters which bubbled up in my not-made-for-walking shoes.

This journey to Santiago had begun a month or so before the actual walk, with an invitation from Kent. He had said, "I'm walking the Camino de Santiago in September; want to go?" At that point the idea of wandering an ancient road some 600 kilometers in length had not entered my mind as something I would do. So I gently declined. Days later the chaos of being told to leave South Africa broke over me. I was only beginning to assess the coming losses when a friend from USAID in Albania asked me to do a "quickie consultation" on human trafficking, and then sail the Adriatic with them for a few days. So I went, realizing that I might not be in these parts of the world again for a long time.

The days in Albania were amazing, as the country was just beginning to open to the rest of the world. The airport still had no windows, and flowers were being planted close to the runway, which looked strangely like a used roadway into town. We drove cross-country from Corfu to Tirana and spent a few days together. My hosts showed me the city and surrounding communities in a lavish manner as one of this couple was the USAID representative there. Her husband was always busy constructing something. I had first come to know them through Pam, who was my U.S. government project officer in Pretoria, South Africa. Many projects on their boat in Corfu and at their home in Tirana filled the space. Amidst the clutter, I couldn't help but notice a magazine titled *Lutheran World*. On the cover was this lead story: "The Road to Santiago: A Journey of Faith." I picked it up, looked at it, and quickly proceeded not to read it.

Psychiatrist and theorist Carl G. Jung described phenomena like my seeing that magazine cover as *synchronicity*. It happens a lot in my life. Synchronicity is the coincidence of events or symbols, albeit unrelated in time and space, seemingly pointing to a singular meaning. First was the invitation from Kent. Then only days later, it was a magazine cover explaining the journey. I thought, *Random, yes, but curious as well. Would I do it?* The reaction was visceral. *NO!*

Leaving Tirana, I took a quick flight down to Athens from where I would depart to Cape Town in the evening. I had 11 hours to burn so I wandered to the Olympic Stadium and the Greek National Museum. The stadium was virtually abandoned a year after the Olympics, and the museum was closed for renovations, maybe a decade or more to complete. So up to the Acropolis and time to gaze at the Parthenon and glorious Greek temples, symbolizing today the greatness and wonder of the roots of Western civilization. After spending hours up there, I walked slowly down, stopping to see the reputed spot where the Apostle Paul preached a sermon (Acts 17:16–34) at the Areopagus (Ares Rock), a place which served as the Court of Appeals in Greek culture. Moved by the possibilities of what such a proclamation as Paul's might mean in the 21st century, I could only find myself lost in wonder and speculation.

It was now getting on toward late afternoon and I was seriously hungry and thirsty since I had been in transit since 5:30 a.m. Stopping in a tavern that was still open late in the day during siesta time, I found the only unoccupied table next to two women caught up in animated conversation. One was Asian and the other African in appearance. They were speaking in English, though. As one spoke plainly to the other, "So tell me about this road or Camino to Santiago?" I withdrew and left the restaurant immediately, as if struck by lightning. The shock of the conversation reverberated within me. For the rest of the day and into the night when we finally left Athens, I found myself feeling that I was being told something, like "walk to Santiago."

A sleepless flight to Cape Town left me exhausted but troubled by this new message of next steps. I stopped by Kent's on the way home. I asked him to explain again his understanding of El Camino and what it entailed. Patiently and yet excitedly, he spelled it out, concluding with, "So, Ted, what do you think? Are you going to do it?" Before I could think I was nodding "Yes" and yet still saying "No" inside. He was delighted. Only a fortnight had passed from the initial invitation and now I was saying, "Yes, I'll do it."

For the next days I was absorbed in selling off my few household goods and in serious preparation for a move to the United States. But Kent continued to challenge me, taking me to a sports equipment warehouse store to purchase the needed all-weather/all-conditions clothing, backpack, and the like. He corrected and cajoled. He instructed and directed. I was going to walk this walk and needed these goods to begin my "practice walking," which was done in the neighborhood on some two miles of Longbeach in Noordhoek every morning at dawn. I wanted to get used to the backpack, the weight, and the movement while traversing the steep beach with sand dunes, mud holes, and seriously big surf.

Kent and I agreed to meet up on the 11th of September in Roncesvalles, Spain, the first stop from St. Jean Pied de Port in the French Pyrenees. Yes, the first day you walk over the Pyrenees into Spain and then the walk begins. Between leaving South Africa and arriving in France, I first stopped in London with a Cape Town clergy friend and his spouse, Chris Chivers and Mary, and their boys, Dominic, Gregory, and Jonathan. Chris was a canon at Westminster Abbey. It was a delight to stay in the Abbey Close and reside where there was an abundance of history and easy access to all of London. To get into shape, I walked up to eight hours daily with a 20-pound backpack through the parklands and along riverbanks, concluding with an epic walk to Greenwich and back up the Thames to Westminster Abbey. Some nine hours of walking which convinced me that I was "in shape" for the journey ahead. And with that I flew down to Biarritz in France and took the milk train for St. Jean Pied de Port for the launch of the journey to Santiago.

Back to my second day on the walk. My questioner was Pascal from Nuremberg. He had been walking the Camino since I began. Later, he would be in that refuge the night of my "outing" as a priest, though he said very little. In his early 30s, he walked with deliberateness and great energy. He welcomed many women into his circle of walkers and chatted them up and occasionally was seen venturing off the road with one or two of them, until he settled on one woman from Estonia, who walked with him through the final two-thirds of the journey. From time to time after the outing he would sidle up to me and quiz me about Jesus, God, or anything spiritual. It seemed to matter to him. As I would learn over time, he was the son of two drug dealers from the 1960s who had settled in the Cape Verde Islands. Upon reaching his 18th year he moved to his homeland of Germany and there took up his citizenship. Working as a mechanic and doing a little drug dealing as well, he was able to make ends meet and live a reasonably comfortable vagabond life.

The previous spring, though, all that changed. He was bicycling through Nuremberg when he was struck by a small truck. It was Holy Week. He had been showing up at the nearby church from time to time, and all he could say on the way to the hospital in the ambulance was, "Please let me walk! Please let me walk!" to no one in particular or perhaps to God, if God was listening. Very weak and somewhat delirious, he recalled the doctors saying, "He will never walk again. He is too damaged and is clearly partially paralyzed." Pascal wept and offered this promise to God that day: "If you let me walk again, I will thank you in Santiago." It was now six months later and he was walking to Santiago.

While I was sitting in a restaurant under the sign "The Way of the Spirit" (Ruela das Animas), Pascal approached. El Camino de Santiago, October 18, 2003.

Throughout the last 20 days of walking he would come and go, appearing and disappearing with great regularity, but upon returning would always bring a new question or concern. I answered as I saw fit and, in a curious way, it drew me out even further with my own musings and speculations: "Who is Jesus for you on this road?" Clearly it was Pascal, whose very name means "liberation" and is another word for Easter. Here he was, his own Easter miracle, walking to Santiago. *Need I see more?* I wondered. Apparently. Some days after our separate arrivals in Santiago, Pascal found me in a pilgrim's restaurant seated under a sign that said "The Way of the Spirit" (in Galician Spanish). He said simply, "I want to know who you know."

Somewhat confused, as it appeared that he knew everyone on the road, I said, "I don't understand. What do you mean?"

"I want to know who you know," he repeated.

"I'm not sure what you are asking."

"It is clear you know Jesus. You talk to him on the road every day. Everyone is aware of it and it is well known that he walks alongside of you. We've all seen him. That's why I keep asking the questions. He keeps answering them through you. So I want to know who you know."

I offered, "Well, if that is the case, it seems that you already do. What can I do?"

"Baptize me. Baptize me tonight."

Dumbstruck, I stuttered a bit, as he was calling out my whole sense of vocation and place within an institution into question. "Well, that would require some time and instruction and a commitment from you to a community of some kind, like a church."

"I know that," he said. "You have already answered those questions, and when I get back to Germany I will do something about that. But I want to know who you know, and the only way to ensure it is for you to baptize me. Tonight!"

I rarely did an irregular, out-of-the-church baptism. And with that understanding, I agreed to do so, at midnight, in the Great Fountain along the side of the cathedral.

When midnight came, he was there with a whole crowd of *peregrinos* from the Camino. I knew a few of them. Carrying candles and singing, they stood around us in a circle while I asked him the core promises of the renunciation from evil, seeking to follow Christ, and pledging his loyalty to the Christian community. Like a child he eagerly took on the promises one after another and embraced the renunciation of his former life. I had purchased a large shell to ladle the water over his head. Three times I poured water in the name of the God the Creator, Christ the Redeemer, and the Paraclete (the Spirit) Life-Giver and Sustainer. Then I anointed him with some aromatic holy oil, which I had secured from one of the priests in the cathedral. With that, he was baptized as a follower of Jesus who is the Christ of God. He smiled and shook with delight, and everyone celebrated with equal energy and enthusiasm. Then, in the full thrall of exuberance, everyone threw water from the Great Fountain on one another in what became a rollicking water fight in the plaza.

At the Pilgrim's Mass in the cathedral the next day, there was Pascal, brave and delighted as you please, stepping forward to receive his first Eucharist as a baptized Christian. On the way back to his seat, he leaned over to me and said, "Thank you. You know, Jesus was with us last night, throwing water as much as you were. Now I know him. I am grateful you got out of the way for me to talk with him on the road. You have modeled how we all need to get out of the way. Thank you."

And with that he disappeared into the crowd in the cathedral. I never saw him again. His candor about seeing Jesus on the road, walking alongside me, was a shock. I have pondered it many times over the years since and have come to this conclusion: The faith I have held across my life got a whole lot bigger the night I baptized Pascal. I moved beyond institutional boundaries. And that is a good thing. I discovered that a long-prayed prayer was finally answered; namely, that I could be transparent or luminous enough to get out of the way for others to see Jesus. What happened out there had nothing to do with me. Pascal already knew that, for he was on a thanksgiving journey, but he encountered more than he bargained for. He found the living faith for which he longed and had a direct experience of the living Christ. Isn't that what many of us are seeking?

Keeping Faith

So what does it mean to keep the faith (Latin, *troth*) and be a person of prayer (Hebrew, *tefillah*)? It is a matter of staying on the road: walking and walking and walking, sojourning until the destination is reached. The challenge is that only God seems to know where that place is or where the Way Stations are to be found. Often it involves getting out of the way to find the Way. The way we learn to live more kindly with one another is to be open to the surprises and wonders of the journey and mystery of the Other. We are invited to live with our hands wide open instead of tightly clenched, and always to be ready to be the eyes, hands, feet, and mouth of something or someone greater than we. I tend toward the Christ. To live kindly is to be kindly and trust that God (or whatever else you may choose to call that possibility of non-local consciousness or the Divine or the Holy) will not let us be harmed, even though we will be hurt by being human. We will also be gifted, it is hoped, with love and acceptance, which are also the givens of our lives. Our challenge is to embrace such truths and live fully in the face of them.

XI

Hope for the Future

The evil in the world comes almost always from ignorance, and goodwill can cause as much damage as ill-will if it is not enlightened. People are more often good than bad, though in fact that is not the question. But they are more or less ignorant and this is what one calls vice or virtue, the most appalling vice being the ignorance that thinks it knows everything and which consequently authorizes itself to kill. The murderer's soul is blind, and there is no true goodness or fine love without the greatest possible degree of clear-sightedness.
—Albert Camus, *The Plague*

I received a random text from Jason in 2016: "So, Casey and I have changed our plans." After a hurried return phone call, I learned that they would not be married in South Beach, Miami, as previously planned, but would be married instead in New Orleans…. On a streetcar, no doubt named "Desire."

Jason—"J"—is a Cajun gentlemen, and Casey, an architect from Buffalo. They had been together for several years and had now proclaimed that their life together was the "real thing" for both of them. We would have to figure out how to make it all happen. I could not help but reflect on the magnitude of the assumptions: You call your best friend's father—who happens to be a priest, whom you have called "mentor" for nearly 20 years—without fanfare or fuss, arrange for your wedding in a different venue, and he's good with it. It is almost a matter of course.

Hold it! It was only some 20 years ago that this same boy called me one evening, at the urging of his best friend—my daughter, Deborah—

and revealed that he was, after all, gay. He asked, as only a 15-year-old can, "Can you help me do this?"

"Of course," I said and then clearly overplayed it with a lengthy discussion about the usual precautions about safer sex, betraying the real worries of any father of a gay son who did not want to see his child at risk. Yet even today I feel the same paternal passion for this man, who has—over the years since—distinguished himself in hundreds of ways in the larger world, and still, he wants me to be present for him and his partner at the most important commitment he has ever made. How far we have come as a community, as a nation, as families, and as a people.

On Labor Day weekend in 2008, while I still worked for WHO,

Celebrating their engagement are Casey Millebrand and Jason Clement in Buffalo, New York, 2016 (photograph by Matt Kinney).

I became part of the growing number of folks involved with the legalization of same-sex marriage in California. I went to Los Angeles, California, from Geneva, Switzerland, and thence to the mountains of central California, 250 miles from the West Hollywood home of a couple named Duncan and John. There they re-committed to their vows, which I had witnessed and officiated in 1993—illegally and without the support of the tradition of the Church—in a carefully crafted "commitment ceremony" in Washington, D.C. These two men had been graduating seniors at George Washington and Georgetown universities. In 2008 they were to be legally married "for the moment" in the State of California. It would be another four years before they would be declared legally married and share the rights of equality under the law with heterosexual Americans, after an appeal to the U.S. Supreme Court overturned the lower court's ruling on Proposition 8. After that, Duncan and John would be legally expected to be spouses forever by their own commitment and to the delight of their two adopted children and hundreds of friends, both in the United States and abroad. In that moment of re-committing, they announced to their gathered community of friends and family that they were able to do this because "Ted showed us how to make our relationship function well and to be engaged in our relationship every day, even when we are angry. We are here today because of him."

Along the way, in this journey toward full rights for same-gender marriage, I have carefully improvised on the liturgies of the Church to bless homes, celebrate unions, and to give witness to the common commitment of two people under God who were held apart from the enjoyment of equal rights. I have also demanded no fewer hours of truth-telling and the usual premarital preparation from gay/lesbian/bisexual/transgender folks seeking commitment than from their opposite-gender counterparts seeking the same. In the meantime, I have defied authority and, rather than ask for permission, have taken the heat of judgment for doing so. Occasionally, I have even had to ask for forgiveness.

Dozens upon dozens of unions, covenants, corporate or limited domestic partnerships, and house blessings have been performed without the overt support of my own Church, which was for much of this time openly arguing my legitimacy as a Christian and particularly as a priest. But as the years have passed and I have kept the faith within reasonable limits, I am grateful to report that the Episcopal Church now blesses same-gender marriages in much the same way it has blessed opposite-gender marriages for centuries; and that, in some dioceses, my Church is represented not only by gay and lesbian clergy like me, but by transgender clergy. Our faith community still strives daily for justice for all people, including refugees, immigrants, and the cast-off refuse of the nations of the world. I am deeply proud to have been both member and participant in this journey to wholeness and holiness.

Across the Anglican Communion, within our nationally indigenous churches, the battle for inclusion and acceptance continues, with losses and victories every step of the way. In large part these churches continue to enact traditions created by their missionary forebears from Europe and the United States. The tragedy of this good work of missionaries is that what they presented as a Gospel in their time is now law and prison in our time. For example, my own beloved Church of Southern Africa, where I was notable among the more out and visible gay and lesbian folk in that Church, challenged my integrity, mission, and purpose before the entire House of Bishops. Each of the 23 bishops had received specially sent documentation of lies and blackmail from vicious detractors claiming to represent the Episcopal Church in the United States. Over the course of two months, and within the context of one-on-one interviews, each asked me, point blank, "Are you here to initiate the American 'gay agenda' on us Africans? Are we really that stupid that you believe that you can do it? And are the Americans that racist to believe that we will accept it?"

I explained that I was there exclusively to care for people with HIV/AIDS, and to recruit and support those who would need such care, as well as those who would render the same. I then testified to each prelate that "Yes, I am a gay man. I am an American. I am a father. I am a son. I am a priest of the Church. And I am a deeply committed and concerned human, fearful of the loss of millions of Africans, and thus the loss of our common humanity." After weeks of one-on-one visits with more than a dozen of my strongest African detractors, I was unanimously supported in my ministry there. The issue never came up again on my watch.

Yet only a decade later the same Church would not support the law of the land in South Africa to bless same-sex unions, and as of this writing regrettably continues to hold that position. The contradictions continue for the human struggle to be whole and to live wholly in every age. Indeed there are victories and defeats. But the struggle remains the struggle for authenticity, dignity, and self-respect.

What began as a struggle for the rights of a few drag queens victimized by the NYPD in the streets of New York City on a sultry summer's evening in 1969 has now *de facto* become the "law of the land" in the United States. By violating civil law and ecclesiastical tradition, and through facing and living into fierce personal opposition, recrimination by civic and ecclesiastical leaders and colleagues, and overt discrimination at the hand of governmental bureaucrats and church administrators around the world, each personal repudiation has effectively become my own badge of honor. It is a privilege to have lived into this journey from self-doubt to self-confidence, from fear to affirmation, from rejection to inclusion, from shame to acceptance, from abhorrence to absolution, and from guilt to grace. Stridently pushing and, when necessary, standing fast, never yielding to political or personal pressure and opening my life to creative resistance.

I have learned that while we can't always see the real outcomes or the victories of our battles for justice, inclusion, acceptance, and respect, each of us in our own way has won those liberties, not with the ease of largesse and privilege, but with an understanding that no matter the cost, what we did/do and why we did/do it was critical for the larger humanity.

The "why" of it? With my own commitment to civil and human rights in the 1960s and then to gay liberation in the 1970s, combined with my ever-deepening engagement within the community living with HIV/AIDS, beginning in 1984, my work started with the simple notion that "no one dies alone." It then was enlarged when I moved into the bigger world to "no one cares alone," and now it has been expanded again to "no one lives in community alone." Like the convergences of movements and communities over the years, we have come a long way and still have farther to go. Nonetheless, I am grateful to have lived through these times.

I think what I am pointing to here is the nature of human hope. Across the pages of this book I have told stories of "how I got over" or what I have lived through. Over and over again I had no assurances or guarantees of what would be achieved by taking a particular position or action. But even in my most lost and confused moments, I found myself in the hands of God, who often was cleverly disguised in the words of a quiet old lady, the observations of a gentleman of faith, in the particularly clear vision of a child, or in the anxious moments of a sick and dying person in a hospice, nursing home, or hospital. No assurances were given per se, just indicators prompted by questions and insights which kept calling me out to stand for a different reality.

I have been fortunate to have lived long enough to see some of my many hopes and dreams become reality. I have also lived long enough to have witnessed unintended consequences of my actions and projects. In each case the enacting of any intervention in the stream of history changes that history, be it for good or ill. But that is the call to responsibility and the claim for acting at all. To say or do nothing is to capitulate to the despair. That I have not done, nor will I. During my time in the Church of St. Thomas in Dallas, I was asked in a television interview during the peak of the AIDS pandemic in the United States what it was like to be in a church where everyone was dying.

I almost took the bait and nearly answered the question with the expected response. But instead I said, "Well, there is no church where everyone is *not* dying. After all, to the best of my knowledge we are all human. But if you are asking me what it is like to serve a community—some of whom are living with HIV/AIDS—then I can tell you that it is a privilege to serve the insistent call of hope. Didn't Jesus of Nazareth serve communities sore afflicted with heartache and pain, poverty and loss, disenfranchisement, and disorder? Yet he proclaimed hope and died for his stance. Is the world a better place because of him? I should think so. Hope is not based on what we have achieved, but what is yet to be achieved, raised up, and celebrated."

The interviewer got more Gospel than he planned and a short homily on hope. But as I think and pray through what is challenging the people of the world with hunger, loss, civil conflict, climate change, human rights, and mass migrations, I am still curiously hopeful. Strident voices for changes are in all of these struggles. Courageous actors have thrust themselves into the crises as agents of change. It seems that what is needed are mentors and guides who can help make the way clearer and show the record of our past failures and gains for similar efforts in order to help these new folk not repeat our mistakes. Mentoring and guiding means that we will not doom the next generation to failure through our silence.

Life is not about getting it "right," whatever that is supposed to mean. Life is about doing life as best we can and with all that we have. Nothing and no one is altogether perfect or bad, for that matter. There is no one solution to anything and everything. Rather, there is showing up and doing what is possible in the moments. All of it, good and bad and indifferent, is part of the larger story, which is God. All of it is part of the greater reality, which is God. Thus nothing and no one can ultimately diminish God or Consciousness by doing. It will all be part of the whole. Our fears and our doubts, our terrors and distrusts are all placed within the context of the larger whole. With this kind of space, God offers each of us a larger view of what it means to be human and humane. In fact, it appears that God is sufficiently big enough to hold opposites. Thus we are called upon to learn forgiveness as one of the

names of God. In Islam there are 99 names of Allah—God. I would sub-
mit to you that *Al-Ghaffar—the repeatedly forgiving*—fills this understanding rather well. Forgiveness, it seems, is needed on a massive scale:
locally, nationally, globally, and universally.

I hope that it has been evident that failure at many things is a universal human experience. Success is often a gift and even a surprise.
Because failure is so prevalent, any person's propensity to fail in relationship is also universal. Only through forgiving one another can we ever
find a way forward. Only through forgiving one's self can we learn true
forgiveness for another as we reconnect to the human flaws of imper-
fection and inconsistency. I have hope because I have come to know the
miraculous power of forgiveness in the very sinews of my being. I can
only testify that while there is heartbreak, turmoil, and loss from any
wound or hurt from another, there is also the ever-present possibility
for wholeness, though it rarely presents itself when we are ready to
accept it. Sometimes we just have to be cajoled into a position to forgive
or be forgiven.

Fortunately, hope is not contingent on any one of us. It is the given
in any challenge or possibility that we may face. But it is a matter of
choosing hope over despair in every moment. I didn't come to life easily
or with facile answers. Answers have never come easy for me. Perhaps
I am hard-headed or maybe slightly less than average? Hard to say.
Regardless, loving, forgiving, and accepting are all I have ever known
to do in the face of contradiction and hardship. I hope it is something
that you can either know, do, or are working toward, no matter where
you are on the journey. *Amen.*

Acknowledgments

Memory is often a moment to get acquainted with the stranger that was you a long time ago. We tell ourselves stories in order to live.—Joan Didion, *The White Album*

Memory fades, memory adjusts, memory conforms to what we think we remember.—Joan Didion, *Blue Nights*

Love's power to restore the broken shards into one whole is the supreme attainment of the human soul.—Frederick Franck., ed., *The Book of Angelus Silesius: 17th-century European Zen Poet*

I have struggled for some years to break my own silences and find the words to tell this story that answers a fundamental question which often haunts my waking and sleeping: *How do we live with one another more gently and with respect?* The heart of any story about a human being often involves struggle, breakdown, and breakthrough; occasionally one remains hopelessly broken. Although there are elements of all of that in this saga, there is also a critical focus on values—a person's principles of worth and standard for behavior in life—as a means of learning and coming to terms with living in our time, and perhaps something worth practicing or using in the times to come. I have found that personal and collective values are a great way to understand life, living, and society. They offer a clarity which overt behavior may not always provide or lead us to emulate. Values are the means by which we explore and artic-ulate meaning. Thus, using the form of the memoir, I have found that exploring these values and the events or stories that inform them is a means of rationalizing, or at least making sense of my life and the living of it. Through the course of writing I learned again that the teaching of forgiveness is essential to carry on life and move to the next level. I hope this book will offer my children and their progeny not just a recollection or a story about their father and grandfather, but a means of living their lives so that integrity and purposefulness may emerge as indicators of who and what they are. Perhaps more importantly, my hope and prayer is that they learn to live with forgiveness, respect and gentleness toward others and particularly within themselves.

The overriding themes of my life have been sojourning and pilgrimage. I have always felt that I was going somewhere, somehow, and then only staying for a spell. Even in retirement I am often asked, "How long are you with us this time?" While the facts are that I have remained rather solitary in Santa Fe for 45 of the 52 weeks in a year, like the one just past, nonetheless I am a sojourner, one who travels away from home, stays for a spell and then returns.

While on pilgrimage to Santiago some years ago, I found myself walking alone and muttering. It had been an exceptionally hard couple of days of walking and I was grousing with the universe in general, noting that I was truly fed up with the journey and the boredom. All at once, a moment of awareness. I had spent nearly 30 years encouraging people to think of life as a pilgrimage—a journey to God, as it were— and now I was on one and I was bored and fed up. Bursting into gales of laughter, I realized that I hadn't reckoned on what a journey of such intensity would mean, especially in the realm of self-conscious reflection. Now I was living it.

A pilgrimage is a journey for a religious purpose and a set destination. It is often understood in context of going to witness some great religious event or to view a religious relic or site, or even to touch or venerate a religious object or take part in a commemorative event, all for the fortification or up-building of the faith. A journey is movement or passage between one place and another. And a pilgrimage is always a journey, but a journey is not always a pilgrimage. Sojourning is to spend time with or in a specific area or place or with a person and then eventually depart for other places or people or even home.

My life is a journey from conception to death and beyond. My consciousness is only historically present for these moments of my human life as "Ted" (or "Teddy"), before becoming part of the consciousness of the world. Thus the journey counts as it brings new experiences and insights about life crucial to the larger consciousness of the whole. An operative metaphor describing spirituality, maturity, theology, or psychology, the journey allows us to see momentum and stagnancy, progress and failure, movement and stasis. It is fair to say that "we are all on a journey." Some of us are on pilgrimages and still others are sojourning in the Now or in the Past. Much of my life has been caught up in trying to meet and read the moment. Everything has been immediate, often with little time for consideration or reflection until the moment has long passed. Thus life comes at me at times with frightening speed and minimal understanding. I am one to often react long before I have a chance to consider reflecting. Occasionally, I have had the gift of anticipation or even preparation, but for the most part, I am reacting in the moment. My life is one long Now. To delight in the luxury of engaging in extensive hind-sighting through writing is a precious gift indeed. Throughout these pages I have sought to tell the whole truth, unvarnished, to the best of my memory. I have introduced an element of reflection and even adjudication.

Using remembered history and moments of confrontation and doubt to tell a story is always risky business. There will be and are memories from others—the actual participants, the nearby observers, and those unseen who may be listening, watching, and recording for posterity—which may be at variance with my telling of the events. I have—in every way possible—sought to verify their understanding of my story by direct communication and their reading of my text. To the best of my understanding I have faithfully recorded the events with all that I am and all that I know. Absolute accuracy cannot be attested to, however. Memory and time, maturity and integrity, emotional capacity, and personal clarity will often alter facts into narrative because personal history is always being rewritten. I have tried to scrupulously explore these moments and their meanings through the entire panorama of a life lived. Thus, I offer this testament as the best that I can do for today, realizing that new material can always be added in the telling.

Many have stood alongside to cheer me on in this endeavor. Among them author Lynn Abbey, my non-biological twin (born at the same hospital in the same moment as I in 1948), who advised, cajoled, and comforted me all along the way; my content and design editor, Eric Wurzbacher, whose insight, precision, and wisdom sustained me in the final push to publication; my copy editor, Jenny Meadows, without whom I would not have found the coherence needed to advance this volume from the beginning. The mystery of words and their sequences have long been my delight and are always the objects of my frustration and contradiction—all at the same time. She has indeed seen and experienced my conflicts firsthand. I am most thankful that she came to me so long ago, when I was still struggling with word and deed. I thank her for her patience and willingness to walk with me all those years!

And always with sincere thanks to my thoughtful and sensitive reviewers: Sue Keith, Cheryl Boots, Mary Elizabeth Moore, Chris Evans, Andy Linscott, B.J. Stiles, Dee McRae, Chuck Walling, Katherine Marshall, Laura Palmer, Edward Moran, Skip Moskey, Marlene Whitehead, Stefan Hippler, Buddy Stallings, Diane Porter, Gene Robinson, Peter Hawkins, Lorraine Tulleken, Jesse Milan, Jr., Jean Duff, Liz Parsons, Dwight Judy, Sandy Thurman, David Schulman, Doug and Martha Puryear, Ron and Dru Ferguson, Larry and Barbara Dossey, Cathleen Crain and Niel Tashima, Kristine Gebbie and Lester Wright, Joel Katz, Joshua and Laura Case, Paula VanNess, William "Bill" Franklin, Sarah Buxton-Smith, Ray Hart and Desmond Mpilo Tutu.

And with very particular love and gratitude to those who have passed from this life to the next—my heavenly watchers are Jerome B. "Jerry" Doster, Don Campbell, William Karpf, Sr., and Nesta; mentors Frances Gibson, Dr. Alice Wonders, the Rev. Drs. George Litch Knight, Joseph C. Weber, and Harrell Beck, the Rev. Dorland R. Russett, Theodore Parker Ferris, Raymond Abbot and Al Kershaw, the Very Rev. Rowan Smith, the Right Rev. Ronald H. Haines, the Most Rev. Edmond L. Browning, Roxanna S. Brewer, Tenn Dyer, Sue Scott, Kathryn Righter, Chakrapani Ullal, my aunt, Jean Evelyn Karpf, and a host of other saints and sinners who have passed over, particularly those who lived and died with HIV/AIDS, and the whole company of ancestors, apostles, martyrs, and seers.

No doubt some of your names are missing, but to you who have loved and supported me through the journeys and sojourns of my life: Thank you.

Bibliography

Buber, Martin. *I and Thou*. Martino Publishing, 2010.

Buechner, Frederick. *The Sacred Journey*. Harper & Row, 1982.

Camus, Albert. *The Plague* [*Le Peste*]. Translated by Stuart Gilbert. Alfred A. Knopf, 1948.

Didion, Joan. *Blue Nights*. Vintage Books, 2011.

Didion, Joan. *The White Album: Essays*. Farrar, Straus & Giroux, 2009.

Eliot, T.S. *Four Quartets*. In *The Complete Poems and Plays: 1909–1950*. Harvest/Harcourt Books, 1943, 1971.

Erikson, E.H. *Identity and the Life Cycle*. International Universities Press, 1959; W.W. Norton, 1980.

Franck, Frederick, ed. *The Book of Angelus Silesius: 17th-century European Zen Poet*. Random House, 1976.

Frost, Robert. "The Death of the Hired Man." In *North of Boston*. Library of Alexandria, 1914.

Habershon, Ada R. "Will the Circle Be Unbroken?" Lyrics, music by Charles H. Gabriel, 1907. Original adaptation by the Carter Family, "Can the Circle Be Unbroken?" released in 1935.

Heschel, Abraham Joshua. *I Asked for Wonder: A Spiritual Anthology*. Samuel H. Dressner, ed. The Crossroad, 2000.

O'Donohue, John. *Anam Ċara: A Book of Celtic Wisdom*. HarperCollins, 1997.

Scott-Maxwell, Florida. *The Measure of My Days*. Alfred A. Knopf, 1968.

Tillich, Paul. *The Shaking of the Foundations: Sermons*. Charles Scribner's Sons, 1948.

Ulanov, Ann, and Barry Ulanov. *Primary Speech: A Psychology of Prayer*. John Knox Press, 1982.

Zittrain, J.L. "The Generative Internet." *Harvard Law Review* 119 (2006): 1974–2004. doi:10.1145/1435417.14354.

Index

Numbers in **bold italics** indicate pages with illustrations experiences during pilgrimage walk 195–205

Carey, the Most Rev. George L. (Archbishop of Canterbury, 1991–2002) 120–121

Chane, the Right Rev. John B. (Bishop of Washington [D.C.], 2002–2011) 115–120 *passim*

children 37, 83, 159, 163, 166, 168–70, 172–73, 184–86; daughter (Deborah) 54, 72, 163–64, 170, 176–81, 183–84, 206–7; granddaughter (Selene) 76, 164, 171, 176–77, 180–81, 183; personal and spiritual debt to 172–73, 184–85; son (David) 54, 72, 157–58, 163–68, 170, 173–177, 183–84, 186; *see also* parenting

Chinnis, Pamela (president of the House of Deputies of the Episcopal Church, 1991–2000) 87, *127*

Church of England 120–21

Church of the Province of Southern Africa (CSPA) *see* Anglican Church of Southern Africa

Clinton, President Bill 118–19

coming out as gay 46–47, 66, 76–77, 79, 121–122, 124, 182; Church reactions to 83, 122–24; excommunication due to 73–74, 126; *see also* gay life experiences

constancy 159, 161, 185; generativity and 162; *see also* generativity

CPSA (Church of the Province of Southern Africa) *see* Anglican Church of Southern Africa

Dallas, Diocese of 83, 133; reprisal and excommunication from 122–23; *see also* Dallas; St. Thomas Episcopal Church

Dallas, Texas: family in 68, 71–75 *passim*; gay community in 82, 145; HIV/AIDS in 54, 66, 67, 70, 83, 85–6, 88, 163; *see also* Dallas, Diocese of; St. Thomas the Apostle Episcopal Church

Davies, the Right Rev. A. Donald (Bishop of Fort Worth, 1982–85) 23, *125*

death and dying (clerical experiences) 156; attending to the dying 22, 66–7, 80–3, 85–6, 143; death of a child 147–56; initial encounter as priest 108–11; HIV/AIDS deaths 54, 59, 95, 111, 122

death and dying (personal experiences) 143, 156: death, life, and the spirit 137–41, 182; God and 138–39, 144–45; illness of daughter 176–81; of mother 41–4, 76–

7; mother's nursing experiences with 111–12; vision of own death 69

Decatur, Alabama experiences 96–9

decent care concept in AIDS and health-care 112

de Vries, C. Michael (Communications Director, World Council of Churches) 51

Dixon, Jane Holmes, (suffragan bishop and interim bishop of Washington [D.C.], 2001–2) 39

Doster, Jerome B. (dying parishioner in Dallas) 80–2, 85–6, 88

dreams: of own death 70; recurrent 19–20; *see also* root dream

Dyer, Dr. John M. (USPHS) 127–28

El Camino see Camino de Santiago

Episcopal Church (U.S.): acceptance and inclusion issues 126, 208–9; clerical obedience owed 124, 125–127; HIV/AIDS work of 30, 88, 130–32; same-sex marriage acceptance 207–10; *see also* Anglican Church of Southern Africa; Anglican Communion; Dallas, Diocese of; St. Thomas the Apostle Episcopal Church; Washington [D.C.], Diocese of; Washington National Cathedral

Episcopal Church (U.S.), personal experiences 163; excommunication 73–74, 126; restoration within 126–27, 131–33; struggles with 23–24, 29, 34, 132–136

Episcopal Church of St. Thomas the Apostle *see* St. Thomas the Apostle Episcopal Church and parish

Erikson, Erik (psychoanalyst on generativity) 158

excommunication 73–4, 124, 126; *see also* obedience to the Church

faith 5, 88, 99, 141–43, 156, 162; calling and 112–13; forgiveness and 26, 29; letting go and 182–86; obedience and 124, 126; parenting and 176, 178, 185–86; prayer and 187–205, 222

Falk, Johanna 147; ministry through loss of their child 147–56

family (birth): aunt (paternal) 32, 55, 131; "Aunt" Marge (Sister Berenice) 191–93; great aunt (Jean; maternal), 209–211; Jewish roots 84–86, 205; parents 19, 24, 32–34, 64–65, 100; violence in 8, 24, 33–35, 50, 162; *see also* abuse in childhood; father; mother; violence in childhood